REALISING THE VALUE OF A BUSINESS

REALISING THE VALUE OF A BUSINESS

A BUYERS' AND SELLERS' GUIDE

BARRIE PEARSON

Livingstone Fisher Associates Plc

Published by Hawksmere Ltd
12–18 Grosvenor Gardens, London SW1W 0DH

British Library Cataloguing in Publication Data
Pearson, Barrie
  Realising the value of a business.
  1. Business firms. Financial management
  658.1'5

ISBN 1 85418 010 X

Printed in Great Britain by Butler & Tanner Ltd,
Frome and London

To the memory of my late parents
. . . Albert and Mary Pearson

The other alternatives available should be considered before deciding to sell a company. Preparatory work needs to be done to ensure that the company is ready to be sold and to make it as attractive as possible to prospective purchasers. Timing the sale is important to get the best price.

Once a decision has been made to proceed with a sale, then prospective purchasers at home and overseas must be identified. The aim is to identify those companies which will derive the greatest benefit, and so are likely to pay the highest price.

Competition is important to obtain the best deal. For the sale of subsidiary companies and divisions, formal auctions are being used more frequently. For a private company, an auction may well be less appropriate but a sense of competitive bidding must be achieved.

Valuation is a matter for truly expert judgement. Scarcity and rarity value, or strategic significance for a particular purchaser, must be recognised because these can enhance the price obtained substantially. None the less, realism is essential. Vendors often have inflated ideas of the worth of their company.

Negotiation is an art not a science. Acquisition negotiation is deceptively complex as well because of the legal and taxation implications. Earn-out deals are a potential minefield to negotiate. There are strong reasons for leaving the lead in the negotiations to be taken by advisers, not least because of the emotional involvement of the vendors. Once oral agreement has been reached, the sale must be carefully nursed through to legal completion.

Expert advice is essential. The choice is confusing. Merchant banks, corporate finance boutiques, business brokers, chartered accountants, management consultants and specialist advisers are possible sources of help and advice.

Loss making companies should be turned round into profit before sale. The effort and delay involved will be handsomely rewarded in terms of the price obtained for the company.

The book has been written to be of benefit to those business owners, group executives, accountants and lawyers who are likely to find themselves involved in selling a company.

A special thank you is appropriate to Anne Garay, who made time to produce a typewritten manuscript from a hand-written one, whilst doing a demanding job as my personal assistant.

Livingstone Fisher Associates Plc
Acre House, 69/76 Long Acre
London WC2E 9JW

CONTENTS

Chapter 1

Chapter 2

Chapter 3

Chapter 4

Chapter 5

Chapter 6

Chapter 7

Chapter 8

Chapter 9

Chapter 10

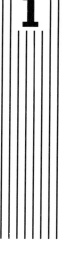

How to Consider Other Options

Many owners of businesses think that the only options to consider are 'to sell, or not to sell'.

There are several other options which should be considered by prospective vendors, even if only briefly. These include:

> ▷ an earn-out deal
>
> ▷ a management buy-out or buy-in
>
> ▷ the sale of a minority stake
>
> ▷ a merger or acquisition
>
> ▷ a stock market flotation

Each of these options will be explained and assessed.

AN EARN-OUT DEAL

An earn-out deal consists of the sale of a business for an initial sum and the opportunity to earn one or more subsequent payments based on the future performance of the company. Earn-out payments are usually based either on the annual pre-tax profit achieved in one or more financial years, or on the

aggregate pre-tax profit achieved over a period
years.

Deals based on sales, gross margin or profit a
normally rejected by acquirers. The use of sales
margin would encourage the vendors to chase growth
expense of profit. If profit after tax is used, there is the p
bility that the amount of corporation tax could be reduc
either by a change in the taxation rules or by the tax expertise
of the purchaser, which means that the vendors would receive
increased earn-out payments from circumstances outside of
their influence.

An actual example of an earn-out deal is:

▷   an initial payment of £7.5 million

▷   plus £0.5 million provided that the profit before tax
in the current financial year is not less than £1.25 million

▷   plus £0.5 million provided that the profit before tax
in the following financial year reaches £1.5 million, and
twice the amount of any additional profit up to a maximum
of £1.75 million profit

This means that the maximum purchase price to be earned
is £9 million.

It must be realised, however, that there is no such thing as
a typical earn-out deal. For example, in a case where the asset
backing is particularly low and profit is expected to increase
dramatically, the percentage of the total price to be earned by
future profit performance may well exceed 50 per cent and in
exceptional circumstances could be about 90 per cent of the
total purchase consideration.

Expert tax advice is needed to ensure that an earn-out is
structured tax effectively for the country in which the deal is
to be done. Pitfalls to be avoided include the risk that the
maximum capital gains tax will become payable on legal completion and the possibility that the deferred payments will be
treated as earned income where this would increase the
amount of tax to be paid.

Earn-out deals are commonplace, especially for service

companies. The main reason is that private businesses are often heavily dependent on the personal contribution of the owners. In the case of a service company, because the net assets of the business may be only a small percentage of the purchase price, this becomes even more important to the purchasers.

Some acquirers underestimate the contribution of the owners, and do so at their peril. Key staff may have stayed with the business because of strong personal loyalty to the owners. Some important customers may continue to buy from the company because of a close acquaintance with the owners and the exceptional personal service provided by them. The goal to be achieved is a smooth transition from a privately owned business to part of a larger group without the unwanted loss of valued staff or customers.

In an earn-out deal, it is normal for the managing director to continue to manage the business throughout the period in which further payments can be earned. If for some reason the present managing director is unable to continue, perhaps because of ill health, then agreement should be reached with the purchasers that one of the other directors will manage the business. The owners will want to manage the business during the earn-out period in order to maximise the amount to be earned.

In most cases, earn-out deals should be arranged for only one or two financial years beyond the current year. This should provide adequate time to replace the owners. If an executive from the acquiring company is to understudy the present managing director for a period, the vendors should establish that the cost of the understudy will be borne by the acquirers to ensure that earn-out payments are not affected.

Sometimes earn-out deals are structured over five or seven years. In the vast majority of cases, this is too long. Acquirers must realise that the vendors will expect considerable freedom to manage the business throughout the earn-out period in a way which maximises the amount they will receive. This means that vendors are unlikely to pursue opportunities which will adversely affect their earn-out payment potential.

Some acquirers naïvely assume that because they do not envisage either diversification or the business making an acquisition itself neither the need nor an opportunity will arise. Sometimes acquirers have become so dissatisfied with the former owners that they have chosen to attempt to negotiate their way out of an earn-out deal and found it an expensive way to gain management control of the business.

Vendors should realise that they are likely to find managing the business for new owners to be frustrating, and the thought of continuing for five or seven years may seem like a life sentence.

The legal contract for the purchase of an unquoted company is likely to be at last thirty or forty pages of double spaced typing. With an earn-out deal the contract could reach ninety pages or more, because there are numerous additional items which may need to be defined in the contract to protect both parties, such as:

▷ accounting policies and auditors

▷ management charges

▷ central services

▷ intra-group trading

▷ provision of finance

▷ dividend policy

▷ cost rationalisation

Each of these items will be explained, and illustrated where appropriate.

Accounting policies and auditors

On legal completion, it must be assumed that the company acquired will be required to change accounting policies to those of the group. This may reduce the pre-tax profits for the purpose of the earn-out deal. Also, the acquirer will wish the group auditors to replace the present ones on legal completion. So the profit figures set for earn-out payments must take into account the accounting policies to be adopted.

In a recent sale it was negotiated on behalf of the vendors that the accounts would be prepared by the present auditors using existing accounting policies during the earn-out period, and then converted into statutory accounts by the group auditors at the acquirer's expense. The reason for adopting this approach was because the advisers to the vendors felt that in this particular case there would be too much scope for subjective differences in the application of group accounting policies.

Management charges

The policy of the acquiring company may be to handle centrally matters such as pension administration, payroll preparation and legal advice. Their procedure is likely to be to make a fixed management charge to each of their subsidiaries for the provision of these services, and the cost involved must be known and agreed.

Central services

It may make sense for the acquired company to make use of central facilities such as the group delivery fleet for distributing goods; sharing the use of regional distribution depots; or using an in-house central publishing department for the production of promotional literature. These services tend to be charged on a usage basis, and it is important to establish the basis and rate of charges which will apply during the earn-out period.

Intra-group trading

The acquired company may be an existing supplier to other subsidiaries within the group. Prior to the acquisition, goods and services will have been provided on an arms-length pricing basis. The acquiring company may have a group policy of 'artificial' transfer pricing between subsidiary companies, which could have a significant effect upon the profits of the acquired company. Equally, there may be a policy requiring subsidiaries to purchase from other companies within the group even if a lower price could be obtained from another supplier outside of the group.

Provision of finance

It is essential to establish that sufficient finance will be available to meet the expansion of the business required to produce sufficient profits for the vendors to benefit from the earn-out potential. If this finance is to be provided by the acquiring company, rather than by an overdraft from a bank, then the interest cost should be defined by reference to the bank base rate.

Dividend policy

It is unusual for an acquired company to be required to pay a dividend to the parent group during the earn-out period. None the less, this needs to be confirmed otherwise borrowings will need to be increased in order to meet dividend payments.

Cost rationalisation

Sometimes it will be agreed that some cost rationalisation will take place following the acquisition, for example the disposal of leasehold premises where two retail outlets would be located too near to each other as a result of the acquisition. It may be desirable to negotiate that all of the costs connected with the disposal will be borne by the acquiring company, so that if these are significantly greater than expected payments to be received under the earn-out deal are not adversely affected.

In the light of the above issues, it will be appreciated that an earn-out deal is much more complex to negotiate than an outright sale of the company. In some cases it may make sense for the vendor to accept a lower amount payable in full on legal completion, rather than the higher aggregate figure which might be obtained under an earn-out deal, because of the uncertainty involved.

MANAGEMENT BUY-OUTS AND BUY-INS

A management buy-out involves members of the management team, backed by one or more institutional investors, buying the company which employs them. In the USA, management buy-outs are often described as leveraged buy-outs or LBOs, because the majority of the purchase price is provided by borrowed money rather than by share capital.

Management buy-outs are commonplace in the UK and the USA, and are increasing in some other European countries. In the UK, buy-out deals have ranged in size from several hundred thousand pounds to several hundred millions, whilst in the USA, the size of the largest deals has increased to several billion dollars.

Management buy-ins usually involve a team of two or three executives, rather than one individual, buying a company in an industry sector in which they have experience, with the financial backing of institutional investors.

Suitable companies

Whether the acquisition is a buy-out or a buy-in, a large proportion of borrowed money will be used to finance the purchase. So there will be a heavy interest burden on the company at the outset. The ability to generate a positive cash flow is essential in order to reduce borrowings. This may involve the sale and leaseback of freehold properties; selling land for residential housing development; or disposing of part of the business as a going concern. Vendors need to identify and assess these opportunities before pursuing a buy-out or buy-in deal, and either set a purchase price accordingly or choose a different disposal route.

Companies with a high net asset backing as a proportion of the purchase price, even in a mature or unfashionable market segment, are suitable because the assets are regarded as security for the borrowing required.

Some service companies are unsuitable for a buy-out or buy-in, because the level of asset backing and the uncertainty concerning future cash flow projections do not satisfy lenders. Businesses which are liable to require injections of cash are likely to be unsuitable, for example a high technology company which requires significant cash during the next two or three years to finance research and development.

Establish the price range

The first step should be to assess what price an acquirer may pay for the business and the likely market capitalisation if a stock market listing is a feasible alternative within the foreseeable future.

Even if a management buy-out or buy-in is an acceptable alternative, other prospective purchasers should be pursued first, or at least simultaneously, in order to ensure an attractive price is obtained.

Handling an approach

Sometimes a buy-in team will make an unsolicited approach to buy the company, 'backed' by a letter from a financial institution offering to support a purchase up to a given value. It must be realised, however, that any instititution invests strictly on the merits of a specific deal and any letter indicating support is far removed from a blank cheque.

A buy-out approach may be made without adequate thought or knowledge of what is involved.

Specific questions to be asked at the outset to those making a buy-out or buy-in approach should include:

▷　how much money are the team committed to invest themselves?

▷　how will they raise the cash?

▷　have they had preliminary meetings with any financial institutions to discuss a possible deal?

▷　what purchase price range do they envisage?

Until satisfactory answers are given, the approach should not be allowed to progress further.

If the buy-out or buy-in is to proceed, the financial institutions will need to receive a detailed business plan. It needs to be established that:

▷　for a buy-out: if agreement to proceed is given, the team will write the business plan in their own time

▷　for a buy-in: only limited time and access will be provided to obtain information needed to write a plan and a confidentiality agreement will be required

When a financial institution has read the business plan and decides to proceed, the management team may be encouraged by them to seek a formal agreement to a period of exclusivity in which to pursue a deal. Furthermore, the advisers to the management team may prompt them to seek a cost indemnity from the vendors to pay their professional costs up to a given limit if a deal is not completed.

Clearly, a period of exclusivity should not be agreed unless other alternative purchasers have been ruled out. Equally, any cost indemnity will be carefully defined and only entered into if it is appropriate.

Once a deal is underway, a timetable to legal completion should be agreed. It is unsatisfactory to allow undue delay because the distraction to the management team, together with the inevitable speculation and uncertainty within the business, is likely to impair performance.

The inevitable outcome

Financial institutions seek to realise their investment in a buy-out or buy-in by a sale of the company or a stock market listing. The majority of institutions aim to achieve this within five years, sooner if possible.

Some vendors have felt cheated when the company has been sold or listed within only a year or two at a much increased valuation. This is another reason why the potential realisable value of the business must be assessed at the outset.

One other possibility which should be considered is for the vendors to retain an equity stake in the company after the buy-out or buy-in in order to participate in any subsequent capital gain.

There is no room for sentiment regarding a buy-out or buy-in. The management team should be regarded as merely another prospective purchaser. The potential value of the business should be assessed at the outset and any deal should be legally completed without undue delay.

THE SALE OF A MINORITY STAKE

Another option to consider is to sell a minority equity stake in the company to one or more financial institutions. This would raise some cash for the existing shareholders and they would retain management control of the business.

Institutions are likely to wish to buy between 10 per cent and 40 per cent of the equity, and would want to avoid having more than 50 per cent of the equity.

Sometimes shareholders sell a minority equity stake or an option to purchase one without sufficient consideration, as part of an arrangement to obtain additional loan finance. Selling equity or granting an option in these circumstances should be regarded as a last resort. If the objective is to obtain loan finance, then every effort must be made to achieve it without disposing of equity on unfavourable terms.

A situation to be wary of is selling a minority equity stake to a competitor. Even before an equity investment is made, commercially sensitive information will have been provided. If the competitor is located overseas, then the information may be less valuable. Careful consideration must be given, however, before any options are granted to increase the investment to give majority control or outright ownership within a given period. Expert taxation advice is required to ensure that granting options will not crystallise any capital gains tax liabilities prematurely and that the risk of undervaluing the worth of the shares at some future date is minimised.

Valuation of a minority stake

It must be realised that the sale of a minority equity stake in an unquoted company of, say, 20 per cent is likely to be valued by a financial institution significantly lower than one-fifth of the price which may be realised by selling the whole company. Their reasoning is that a minority equity stake gives them little influence over the management of the company, even with the appointment of a non-executive director, and that the only opportunity to sell their minority stake may be to the other shareholders; unless the company is sold or obtains a stock exchange listing in due course. Consequently, it is important to approach three or four financial institutions at the outset to establish their interest and to obtain an indication of their valuation, before deciding to proceed in earnest with any one of them.

Appointment of a non-executive director

Institutions investing in the equity of an unquoted company will usually require the appointment of a non-executive director nominated by them. The person nominated is likely to be someone from their 'pool' of non-executive directors or, possibly, an executive from the instititution.

Unquoted companies tend to respond emotionally to the thought of having a non-executive director appointed by a financial institution on their board. It is not as bad as it may appear at first thought, and could prove helpful.

The institution should be asked to nominate someone who will add something to the skills of the board. For example, a knowledge of the business gained from experience at either the supplier or customer end of the chain or some relevant technical expertise, such as foreign currency management, if this is an important feature of the business. If the first person put forward does not appear to fit in acceptably with board members, the institution should be asked to put forward an alternative candidate.

As well as carrying out a monitoring role on behalf of the financial institution, the non-executive director should be expected to bring a more structured approach to board meetings, offer a wider perspective on what is happening in the industry sector, and have some useful personal contacts amongst prospective customers and suppliers.

Eventual sale of the company

Many financial institutions will seek to realise their equity investment by a sale of the company or a stock market listing within about five years. If the wish is to obtain a long-term equity investment, then this should be discussed openly with prospective investors in the initial meetings.

One factor to be aware of is the possible problems created by having an outside investor when the time comes to sell the business. There have been cases where the financial institution has exerted considerable pressure to reject an offer which the remaining shareholders would have been quite happy to accept.

The sale of a minority equity stake may be an appropriate alternative if the objective is to release some cash for the shareholders whilst maintaining management control. It could be particularly appropriate if the goal is to achieve a stock market listing within the next five years, because the minority equity investment would accelerate the introduction of the disciplined approach required by a stock market listed company. The trap to avoid, however, is the sale of a minority equity stake or the granting of an option at a price which subsequent performance reveals was far too low.

MERGER

There need to be strong reasons to justify two privately owned companies choosing to merge, which means that the two companies are joined into one without any exchange of cash.

Valid reasons

Some valid reasons to pursue such a merger could be:

▷ to accelerate a stock market listing by achieving the requisite level of profit more quickly

▷ to achieve the size of business required to support the minimum level of infrastructure needed to compete effectively, for example to afford the level of new product development required by a computer software company

▷ to reduce dependence on one product or service, or on only a few customers

▷ to avoid the outright sale of a company on unfavourable terms arising from a death, serious ill health or enforced retirement

Management

The future direction, priorities and aspirations of the merged business must be agreed at the outset, otherwise there is no point in pursuing a merger.

There is the strongest possible case for agreeing that there will be one managing director after the merger, and not joint ones, to avoid unnecessary disagreement. Both the principle and the choice of individual need to be agreed next.

The board members and their roles need to be agreed. Responsibility and accountability for particular functions such as marketing or sales cannot be shared effectively. One person must be given individual accountability.

Another issue which should not be underestimated is the problem of harmonising salary levels, fringe benefits and conditions of employment without causing a significant increase in costs.

Also any relocation of offices or factory is likely to be time consuming and costly. Even the cost of a change of name should not be underestimated in terms of product literature, vehicle livery, stationery and so on.

Valuation

Failure to agree a valuation may well negate any real hope of achieving a merger.

The objective must be to agree the percentage of the merged company that each set of shareholders will own. This has to be achieved without the existence of a market price for the shares in either company to provide a benchmark.

Profit is almost certain to be the relevant basis, rather than net asset values shown on the balance sheets. The problem is likely to be, however, that the two companies will have different rates of profit growth both to date and projected for the future. This means that disagreement is probable concerning the relative values of the two companies.

Overall, a merger of two privately owned companies should be avoided unless there are strong reasons for doing so. Even then, an acquisition of one company by the other, for shares or cash, may prove to be the only feasible alternative.

STOCK MARKET FLOTATION

In the UK, there are three markets regulated by The Stock Exchange for companies seeking a quotation for their shares.

These are:

▷ The Official List

▷ The USM (Unlisted Securities Market)

▷ The Third Market

The main difference between the three markets is the size of the companies whose shares are quoted upon them. So the first requirement is to check that the profit of a company is sufficient to be suitable for a quotation.

The Official List

The Official List is the main market regulated by The Stock Exchange.

The pre-tax profits reported for the most recent financial year should exceed £1 million to justify entry, otherwise a USM listing may be more appropriate.

The company needs to have at least a five-year trading record, and a minimum of 25 per cent of the equity will need to be held by outside shareholders.

The USM

The Unlisted Securities Market is widely referred to as The USM. It was launched in 1980 to encourage the flotation of smaller companies. Since then over 600 companies have joined The USM, and more than 100 of these have graduated to a full listing on the main market.

The pre-tax profits reported for the most recent financial year should exceed £500,000 to justify the expense involved and to provide a sufficient market in the shares. Although only 10 per cent of the shares of USM companies need to be held by outside shareholders, it has been common for the proportion to be about 25 per cent in order to create a sufficient market in the shares.

The company needs to have a three-year trading record; but where funds are required for a fully researched new product or project then the lack of trading record may be acceptable.

The Third Market

Trading in The Third Market commenced in 1987, to provide an opportunity for companies with a one-year trading record or 'greenfield situations' to obtain a share quotation. About fifty companies have joined The Third Market, and a handful have moved up to The USM.

The pre-tax profits reported for the most recent financial year by an established company should exceed £200,000 to justify the expense involved and to provide some market in the shares.

Suitable companies

It is not sufficient merely to have reported an acceptable level of profit to be a suitable company to obtain a share quotation. A sponsor, either a stockbroker or merchant bank, is needed. Suitable management and future profit growth must be demonstrated. There should be no serious question marks concerning the business or the directors.

The sponsors will have to be convinced that the company is suitable for a stock market quotation, because their reputation is at risk. They will want to be satisfied that:

▷ the company has a satisfactory record of profit growth during recent years

▷ adequate budgetary control, profit forecasting and cash management exist to ensure that current year forecasts are reliable

▷ the profits will continue to grow at an acceptable rate during the next two or three years and the company has a long-term future

▷ the company is not unduly dependent on one person, and there is demonstrable management competence

▷ if the company has only one product or service, there is not undue vulnerability to changing demand or competition

▷ the company is not unduly dependent on a mere handful of customers or clients

▷ a suitably qualified accountant is employed as finance director

▷ a medium-sized or large firm of chartered accountants are auditors to the company

▷ the directors and major individual shareholders wish to continue their commitment to the company by retaining a substantial proportion of their shareholding

▷ the corporation tax, PAYE, and VAT affairs of the company are in order and up to date

▷ adequate working captial is available for the growth and development of the business

▷ there is no threat of litigation hanging over the company

Benefits of a share quotation

There are benefits to be gained by shareholders, directors and staff, including:

RETAINING MANAGEMENT CONTROL

The major shareholders will have the opportunity to sell up to about a quarter of their shares and still retain management control of the company.

ESTABLISHING A MARKET IN THE SHARES

A realistic market price will be created for the shares, which may be substantially higher than the prices at which occasional sales and purchases of shares have taken place previously. Also, small shareholders will be able to buy and sell shares more readily.

RAISING FINANCE

Additional avenues of raising finance become available. More shares can be sold in the future, probably by a rights issue to existing shareholders. As a quoted company, financial institutions will be prepared to underwrite a share issue so that there is no obligation upon existing shareholders to subscribe for additional shares.

As there is a market for the shares, the issue of more shares can be used to pay for acquisitions. Whilst it may be unacceptable for the vendors to receive the purchase consideration wholly or partly in shares, it should be possible to place blocks of shares with financial institutions to raise the cash required.

STATUS AND AWARENESS

Some private companies dealing with multinational customers and suppliers have a problem of financial credibility. There is evidence to show that a stock market quotation has been of significant help in creating an adequate financial status.

The press coverage leading up to a share quotation, and the continuing interest afterwards, is likely to increase awareness of the company significantly.

MANAGEMENT AND STAFF MOTIVATION

There is no doubt that the flotation of a company creates excitement amongst management and staff. There will be an opportunity for staff to buy shares at the time of flotation, or to sell a proportion of their existing holdings. A share option scheme can be introduced at the same time to create a wider involvement in the future success of the company.

Disadvantages of a share quotation

The amount of preparatory work involved and the continuing requirements for a quoted company should not be under-estimated. The disadvantages of flotation include:

PREPARATORY WORK

The scrutiny of the company, and its future prospects, by

the sponsors and the reporting accountants is time consuming for the directors.

The reporting accountants will produce what is known as a long-form report examining:

▷ previous financial results for up to five years

▷ the history, business, prospects, management, and financial performance of the company and each subsidiary

▷ management information and control systems, organisational structure and management succession

▷ service contracts, pension schemes and benefits in kind

▷ the forecast financial results for the current year

▷ the adequacy of working capital to meet the anticipated needs of the business

The writing of the prospectus to accompany the share quotation must be the subject of meticulous attention to detail to ensure that the information is accurate.

It is desirable that only one or possibly two directors are closely involved with the provision of information for the long-form report and the prospectus. Otherwise, there is a real risk that the performance of the business will suffer during the vital period leading up to the flotation, which could undermine the achievement of the pre-tax profit forecast for the current year.

THE SIX-MONTHLY TREADMILL

In the UK, quoted companies are required to report their financial results for six-month periods. In the USA, quarterly reporting of results is commonplace.

Stock market analysts and financial journalists compare the results achieved for the first half of the financial year with the corresponding period in the previous year, as well as making a similar comparison for the full year performance. Without doubt, this does create additional pressure on the directors, management and staff of the business. Whilst capital expenditure and revenue expense need to be invested to ensure medium-term profit growth, there is still the requirement to produce an acceptable result every six months.

DIVIDEND PAYMENTS

As a private company there is no requirement to pay a dividend at all. For a quoted company, however, investors will have a definite level of expectation related to the size, type of business and future prospects of the company. It is quite typical for between one-third and one-half of profits after tax to be paid out as dividend to the shareholders in a quoted company. This is a significant drain on cash flow which cannot be ignored.

PUBLIC SCRUTINY

The directors of some private companies enjoy indulgences provided by the businesses which will be completely unacceptable to the sponsors. These may include a boat, an aeroplane or helicopter, an overseas villa, and racehorses. Some members of the families of directors may receive a salary and a company car, without having a commensurate job in the company. This sort of thing often amounts to nothing more than using a company to finance an extravagant lifestyle, in a way which is totally unacceptable when outside shareholders are involved.

INFORMATION DISCLOSURE AND CONTINUING OBLIGATIONS

There must be timely disclosure of half-yearly and annual financial results to The Stock Exchange. Also, various other situations need to be notified.

Annual General Meetings have to become a formal and public occasion, requiring preparation to handle contentious issues which may be raised by those attending.

Directors are not allowed to buy or sell shares at various financially sensitive times during the financial year.

MEDIA ATTENTION

Journalists need stories, favourable and unfavourable. As a private company, it is probable that a story would not appear in the press at all, or only in local newspapers, and would not affect the share price.

For a publicly quoted company the situation is likely to be quite different. The sudden resignation of a founding director or the sale of a substantial part of a personal shareholding may not only be reported in the financial press but have a significantly adverse impact on the price of the shares as well.

The costs of flotation

The cost of obtaining a share quotation depends upon the method chosen. Three options are available. These are:

▷ an introduction

▷ a placing

▷ an offer for sale

AN INTRODUCTION

The required percentage of shares to be held by outside investors may have already existed amongst a reasonably large number of shareholders for a considerable time. If so, then an introduction is sufficient and a full prospectus will not be required.

An introduction is the lowest cost method of obtaining a quotation, and depending upon the amount of public relations work decided upon, the cost will probably be less than £100,000. As additional finance is not being raised, the costs of an introduction will have to be met from within the business.

A PLACING

A placing involves the sponsor selling the shares to be made available to financial institutions and private clients. This has been the most common method for USM entrants, and is increasingly used for smaller companies joining The Official List.

The maximum amount which may be raised by a placing on The USM is £5 million, and for The Official List is £15 million. Higher amounts require the use of an offer for sale.

The cost of a placing on The Third Market is likely to be in excess of £100,000, and in the region of £200,000 for The USM. The figure will be considerably higher for a placing to join The Official List, and a full prospectus will need to be published in a national newspaper if more than £2 million worth of shares is being sold. The costs of the placing will be met from the cash raised by the sale of new shares.

AN OFFER FOR SALE

An offer for sale is made by press advertisement and by inviting purchasers to apply for shares on the application form included at the end of the prospectus.

The offer for sale is most appropriate to substantial companies joining The Official List. The minimum cost may well be £500,000 and for a large issue could be many times this figure. Once again, the costs will be met from the proceeds of the offer for sale.

Provided that the pre-tax profit is large enough and the company is a suitable one for a share quotation, the benefits outweigh the disadvantages. It must be said, however, that a substantial amount of preparatory work and cost is involved. The continuing demands and regulatory framework upon the directors is also considerable. Above all, it must be recognised that there will only be an opportunity to sell about a quarter of the equity at the time of the share quotation, and key shareholders will be expected to retain the bulk of their remaining shares for some considerable time.

EXECUTIVE SUMMARY

Consider alternative options to a sale:

> ▷ earn-out deals:
> - require detailed negotiation and careful definition

> ▷ management buy-outs and buy-ins:
> - regard them as only another prospective purchaser
> - consider retaining an equity stake in future success

> ▷ sale of a minority equity stake:
> - releases some cash and retains management control
> - realises less than a pro rata price compared to outright sale

▷ merger:
- means no cash changes hands
- needs strong reasons to justify it

▷ stock market flotation:
- requires a suitable business and management team
- needs sufficient pre-tax profits to justify entry
- shareholders must retain a substantial stake after flotation

How to
Choose the
Time to Sell

2

Many people delay too long before selling a business. Perhaps a more accurate word is procrastinate rather than delay. What is more, large groups disposing of a subsidiary are just as guilty as privately owned businesses.

The stimulus for the disposal of a subsidiary is sometimes an approach by the management team wishing to pursue a buy-out deal or from another group wishing to buy the business. The question of continued ownership of those subsidiary companies which are not an essential part of the core business of the group, however, should be reviewed regularly, probably annually. It is important to look at the prospects for each subsidiary during the next five years in arriving at a decision to dispose of it or not.

TIMING RISKS

Key factors which must be anticipated during the next five years include:

▷ sharply increased competition, including entrants from overseas and different competitors at home, eg the committed entry of supermarket chains in the UK for the sale of wines and spirits during the 1980s

▷ forthcoming legislation and the impact it will have on the business, eg the impact of the Financial Services Act during 1988 in the UK on independent intermediaries which provide investment advice to private clients

▷ technological change, eg the growing replacement of individual typewriters by integrated word processing systems

▷ inherent over-capacity in the industry within the medium term, eg certain sectors of the shipping industry worldwide

If there is likely to be a serious decline in profitability in a subsidiary within the next five years and it is not a core business, then disposal of the business now should be evaluated.

Probably the worst situation which can be allowed to happen is when a business is making losses and needs substantial capital expenditure to restore profitability. If this happens, the business may well be unsaleable in the short term.

When considering the sale of a privately owned company, there are personal factors to be considered in addition to the commercial issues outlined above.

The statistical evidence is overwhelming. People aged over 45 face a substantially increased risk of prolonged illness and sudden death. If the business is particularly dependent upon one person, then a prolonged illness or death may significantly reduce the amount a purchaser is prepared to pay, or even dissuade him from buying the company.

People naïvely assume that prolonged illness and sudden death only happen to others and that future results will show uninterrupted progress.

A major concern of any purchaser is that the vendors are selling because the business has reached a peak. So a reduction of the pre-tax profit in the previous year, or the forecast for the current year, is likely to make a purchaser distinctly nervous. Even a pre-tax profit plateau will cause concern. Some prospective purchasers will take the view that it is better to delay the purchase until profit growth has been demonstrably restored, and will then be prepared to pay a higher price for the business.

TIMING OPPORTUNITIES

It would be short-sighted simply to aim to avoid selling the business at an unfavourable time.

The aim must be to spot timing opportunities. These may be quite short-lived, perhaps no more than a couple of years, and yet they provide the opportunity to sell a business at a higher price.

One recent example of this in the UK involves independently owned chains of estate agents having more than twelve branches. During the previous two years several major companies, including Lloyds Bank and Prudential, had purchased numerous estate agencies to create national chains. Other companies, particularly other financial institutions, have realised belatedly that estate agencies are an important distribution outlet for mortgage finance and endowment life assurance. A temporary result has been the purchase of some of the remaining chains of estate agents at substantially increased prices.

The increased competition in the market-place which is likely to follow this spate of acquisitions may well reduce the profitability of smaller chains of estate agents within the medium term. By this time, the appetite to make further acquisitions is likely to have reduced sharply as the major chains concentrate on selective organic growth. The net result could well be that some of the smaller chains will wish they had taken the relatively short-lived opportunity to sell at a temporarily high price, which may not be achievable again for several years.

Another example is the high level of acquisition activity in certain European countries in some sectors as a prelude to the creation of a single European market by 1992. Careful timing is needed to ensure that a disposal is not made prematurely, before scarcity or rarity value becomes a reality as the number of acquisition targets diminishes.

SHORT-TERM TIMING OPPORTUNITIES

Within a financial year, a favourable time to be negotiating the sale is towards the end of the year, when the profit forecast looks fairly certain to be achieved.

The purchase price should be negotiated on the strength of the profit forecast, and not the actual figure for the previous year. In contrast, after four months of a financial year, a purchaser will regard the audited accounts as merely confirmation of the results for the previous year, and disregard the management accounts for the first quarter of the current year as too early to provide a sound basis for a full-year profit forecast.

THE TIME REQUIRED

For a group disposing of a subsidiary, the time required is merely the time for essential preparatory work to be carried out and then legally to complete the transaction.

For a privately owned company, however, it may well be several years after the deal is legally completed before the directors are able to withdraw from the management of the business.

For owners, the time required to withdraw from the business completely increases down the following list:

▷ management buy-out
▷ management buy-in
▷ outright sale
▷ earn-out deal
▷ stock market flotation
▷ sale of minority stake
▷ merger with another unquoted company

Each of these alternatives will be considered in turn.

Management buy-out

Venture capitalists publish case histories illustrating particular buy-out deals which have been legally completed in three months, and no doubt those ones were. In practice many buy-out deals are allowed to take much longer to complete from the time of the original decision to sell the company.

In order to obtain the highest price, the buy-out team must simply be regarded as one of several prospective purchasers. This means that either preliminary talks should be held with other prospective purchasers before, or at least simultaneously with, the buy-out team being given the authority to release their business plan to institutions.

For the disposal of a subsidiary, it may be appropriate to have a full prospectus for sale written by professional advisers and an auction carried out to a strict timetable. Before the prospectus is issued to prospective purchasers, however, several months may be needed to deal with preparatory work such as:

▷   deciding which overseas operations are to be included in the disposal, such as sales offices

▷   tidying up the statutory structure of the business for ease of separation

▷   considering the taxation implications involved

▷   establishing the pension fund entitlement of those people employed in the subsidiary

▷   transferring properties into or out of the business to be disposed of, as appropriate

▷   transferring intellectual property such as patents and trade marks or granting a licence for the use of them, as appropriate

Overall, it would be realistic to allow four to six months, and certainly not more than twelve months, to complete a disposal by a buy-out deal. One thing is certain, however: once a management team have been given the authority to proceed, they should be expected to adhere to an agreed timetable. The business will suffer from a lack of attention from the management team during the period leading up to the legal completion of a buy-out, and it must be accepted as inevitable that rumour and uncertainty will be widespread throughout the business. Worse still, if rumours of a deal spread prematurely outside of the company then the business could be further damaged.

In a recent buy-out from a multinational engineering company, the deal was allowed to drift for almost three years from the initial discussions with the management team to legal completion. Such a situation is totally unacceptable and unnecessary.

Management buy-in

As with a buy-out deal, a buy-in should not be allowed to take more than six months to reach legal completion.

In addition, however, it is possible that the new management team would wish for some part-time consultancy help to be available on request for the first few months to ensure a smooth change of ownership.

Outright sale

Before the sale process even commences, it has to be established that now is a sensible time to sell the business.

After a profit setback, some vendors want to sell too quickly. Consider a business which has had a record of several years of uninterrupted profit growth until the previous year, when profits fell sharply or a loss was incurred. Prospective purchasers are unlikely to be convinced when offers for the business are invited based on the strength of a return to profitability in the first quarter of the current year and projections of a rapid return to record levels of profit.

In such circumstances, the professional advisers to the vendors should be challenging the desire to sell now instead of in, say, two years' time. By then, it should have proved that the recent year was merely a temporary hiccup, and not the beginning of a period of uncertain profitability.

Serious litigation in progress, or perhaps worse still the threat of possible litigation, needs to be resolved before the sale of the business commences. Equally, a major dispute with the Inland Revenue or an investigation by them may need to be dealt with before selling the business. In these matters two years is not an unreasonable length of time to clear matters up.

For the disposal of a subsidiary by selling to a corporate buyer, preparation work needs to be done similar to that described earlier for a buy-out deal, which could require several months.

For the sale of a private company, however, the price to be obtained may be increased substantially by a lengthy period of preparation, as outlined in Chapter 4. During the two years prior to a sale, the aim should be to demonstrate attractive profit growth and to present a well-managed company to prospective purchasers, with future growth opportunities already being pursued.

The actual sale process is likely to take at least six months, probably significantly less for an auction based on a detailed prospectus for sale, but it would be sensible to allow up to twelve months.

These periods are based on the following estimates:

	Sale	Auction
Month 1	Write brief synopsis; research prospective purchasers	Write detailed prospectus
Month 2	Approach prospective purchasers; hold initial meetings with them	Announce auction; invite outline bids

Month 3	Arrange visit to company by each short-listed purchaser	Negotiate with short-listed purchasers
Month 4	Negotiate to reach verbal agreement	Accountancy investigation and legal completion
Months 5/6	Accountancy investigation and legal completion	

It must be recognised that:

▷   a decision to auction should presuppose that an acceptable offer will be obtained, because otherwise the publicity will adversely affect the company, especially if it is a subsidiary, and in this case a failure to sell may damage the credibility of a vendor group which is listed on a stock market

▷   in the case of a sale, it is possible that a prospective purchaser will withdraw the offer or reduce it unacceptably as a result of the accountancy investigation, and do so only shortly before legal completion. Detailed negotiations then are needed with another prospective purchaser who has been kept in reserve

▷   holiday seasons such as summer, Christmas and the New Year can easily add another month to the above timescales

With the sale of a subsidiary, the deal will almost certainly be a 'clean break' one. In contrast, it is highly probable that the key directors of a private company will be required either to sign service contracts for a period of at least a year or to provide part-time consultancy services for several months to ensure a smooth transition to new ownership.

If all goes smoothly, the sale of a privately owned company can be legally completed within six months, but up to twelve months may be needed.

In both cases, if the timing to sell is wrong or if there is a cloud hanging over the company, up to two years may be needed before selling.

In addition, for private companies the key directors should expect to be required to continue in a full-time capacity for at least a year, or at least to provide part-time consultancy help for several months. So it makes sense to consider seriously an outright sale of a company between one and five years before a clean break can be achieved.

Earn-out deal

The time required for the legal completion of an earn-out deal should be similar to that for an outright sale.

The period of executive involvement by the vendors after legal completion may be significantly longer, however, than in an outright sale. This is particularly likely to be the case if:

> ▷ the asset backing is less than, say, about 25 per cent of the aggregate purchase price, and/or

> ▷ future success could be adversely affected by the loss of one or more major clients, and/or

> ▷ the business is significantly dependent upon the personal expertise or contribution of one or more of the vendors, and/or

> ▷ there is inherent uncertainty about the future profits because of outside influences such as possible legislation or major technological development affecting the industry sector

Most earn-out deals extend for only one or two years beyond the current financial year. In exceptional cases, however, the earn-out payments have covered a five, or even seven-year period. This would mean that prospective vendors should be considering a sale between seven and ten years before they wish to retire from the business.

Stock market flotation

Whilst the process of flotation can be achieved in about six months, this assumes that the groundwork has already been completed. In reality, this may require up to two years in order to:

▷ appoint suitable auditors and have them produce at least one set of annual accounts prior to flotation

▷ create a suitable corporate and statutory structure for the business

▷ recruit a qualified finance director

▷ appoint a suitable chairperson and at least one other non-executive director

▷ ensure the tax affairs of the company are up to date and that tax planning arrangements are made for the major shareholders

▷ create an employee share option scheme

After flotation, those directors having a significant share-holding will be expected to continue their full-time executive role for several years. So, once again, it is necessary to think up to seven years ahead of the envisaged time of withdrawal from the business.

Sale of a minority stake

The sale of a minority equity stake may well be legally completed in three to six months from the decision to pursue this route.

The new investors will assume that the present management are to continue. So, in essence, the eventual sale or flotation of the business has not really commenced yet.

Merger with another unquoted company

The merger should be completed within six to twelve months of selecting this alternative. Also, a feature of the deal may be that one or more of the shareholders will have the opportunity to retire from the business almost immediately.

The remaining directors will be further away from a sale or flotation than in any of the other situations described above. Either a prospective purchaser or a sponsor for a stock market flotation is likely to want to wait for at least a year after the legal completion of a merger to be satisfied that the integration work has been completed successfully and that future profit growth can be predicted safely.

EXECUTIVE SUMMARY

Think about disposal early:

▷ for a subsidiary—up to five years ahead

▷ for a private company—at least seven years before planned retirement

Do the preparatory work anyway to be ready to:

▷ obtain a stock market quotation quickly when conditions are particularly favourable

▷ sell at short notice when inflated prices are being paid temporarily

Consider the sale of a declining business well before losses occur.

How to Choose and Use Advisers

Outside help may be costly, and there can be no guarantee that a deal will result.

In order to decide what outside advice and help may be needed, or beneficial, it is necessary to identify the tasks to be done and the expertise required.

The tasks to be done include:

▷ identifying the options available, both now and in the foreseeable future

▷ choosing the preferred option to pursue

▷ preparing the company to obtain the best deal possible

▷ carrying out the tax planning

▷ valuing the business

▷ deciding the price to seek and the minimum to accept

▷ identifying prospective purchasers, investors, or sponsors as appropriate

▷ approaching them to establish a definite interest

> ▷ negotiating the deal

> ▷ handling the legal work to complete the deal

The types of expertise required are:

> ▷ strategic

> ▷ taxation

> ▷ valuation

> ▷ negotiation

> ▷ legal

A general knowledge of these subjects is likely to prove woefully inadequate, and expensive. First hand and up-to-date knowledge and experience of each particular subject in connection with acquisitions and disposals is essential.

The need to be 'up to date' must not be underestimated. In the twelve months after the wordwide stock market fall of October 1987, the relative prices of unquoted acquisitions soon fell significantly, but within six months some sector prices were at least as high as before the fall because of a scarcity of acquisition targets.

With regard to the taxation of earn-out deals in the UK, the Inland Revenue announced an Extra-statutory Concession in April 1988, which had a significant impact on the most tax effective way to structure deals.

Most people agree with the need for expertise in handling the taxation, valuation and legal aspects of a disposal. Negotiation is viewed differently. Many business people believe themselves entirely capable of negotiating the sale of their own business.

This could be a dangerous assumption. The negotiation of a disposal is commercially complex, and it must be done with an awareness of the tax and legal considerations which will inevitably follow. What is more, people become emotionally involved. They may well be insulted by what is considered to be too low an offer. Tempers may become frayed.

There is just as strong a case for needing expert negotiation skills as for taxation, valuation and legal work. Indeed, skilful negotiation may increase the price obtained significantly and even make the difference as to whether or not a deal is completed at all.

The sources to find the expertise required should be:

▷ firstly, from within the company

▷ if not, from existing advisers

▷ lastly, from different advisers

Each of these options will be considered in turn.

WITHIN THE COMPANY

It is not enough to assume that the existence of a business development, legal, taxation or financial analysis department means that the requisite expertise is available.

Specific questions must be answered satisfactorily:

▷ does the business development department have sufficient and up-to-date knowledge to assess which other alternative options could be feasible?

▷ does the legal department have recent acquisition and disposal experience? Can they give the speedy attention required?

▷ does the tax department have someone with the requisite and specialised corporation tax, capital gains tax and VAT expertise?

▷ does the financial analysis department have someone with up-to-date valuation expertise and a thorough knowledge of earn-out deals, based on practical experience?

Otherwise, outside advice should be obtained.

EXISTING ADVISERS

The next source to be considered should be existing advisers. If they have the requisite expertise, it must make sense to consider using them before approaching different advisers.

The existing advisers will include a firm of chartered accountants, acting as auditors, and probably solicitors. One should not assume, however, that all firms of accountants and solicitors will have the requisite expertise.

The firm should be asked:

▷ is there at least one partner who specialises in this work or at least is involved regularly with it?

▷ what deals has the person completed during the past twelve months? How large and complex were these? Who were the advisers to the other side?

▷ is it possible to meet the person concerned? (unless he or she is already known)

Most sizeable towns are likely to have at least one firm of accountants and solicitors with one or more specialists in acquisition and disposal work. What is more, they are likely to be significantly less costly than major firms in large cities.

DIFFERENT ADVISERS

If it is necessary to choose different advisers to obtain the requisite expertise, there are two problems to be faced:

▷ which type of adviser to choose?

▷ how to pick a particular adviser?

The different types of adviser include:

▷ chartered accountants

▷ solicitors

▷ business brokers

▷ merchant and investment banks

▷ acquisition and disposal specialists

Each one of these will be considered in turn.

Chartered accountants

Most large firms of chartered accountants have at least one separate corporate finance department in each country. Their regional offices are likely to have one or more partners who handle acquisition and disposal work.

Medium-sized firms should have at least one partner in each office with experience of acquisition and disposal work. It is likely, however, that this work is only handled intermittently as part of a wider audit role within the firm. Like large chartered accountants, medium-sized firms should have specialist tax partners to provide the taxation expertise required.

It is the small firm, perhaps two or three partners operating in a small town, which could be a cause for concern. Their involvement in acquisition and disposal work of any complexity may be virtually non-existent, or at best intermittent. It is unlikely that one of the partners is a full-time tax expert, so even the requisite tax expertise may not be available.

It is understandable that a small firm would like to have the opportunity to handle a disposal. At the risk of offending small accounting firms, however, it has to be said that positive proof of their experience is required. A psychological disadvantage which a partner in a small firm may have, even if technically competent, is being faced with prestigious advisers representing the other side. This is a real factor, which must be considered.

Solicitors

Large firms of lawyers in major cities are likely to have specialist departments handling acquisition and disposal work. Smaller firms in sizeable towns may have at least one partner handling acquisitions and disposals fairly regularly. The small law firm is likely to have the same shortcomings and dis-advantages as the small accounting firm.

Some firms of lawyers offer one-stop shopping. In addition to the legal work, they may suggest that they handle the nego-tiation and taxation aspects as well. At the risk of being accused of having a conservative and even old-fashioned outlook, once again positive proof is required.

Business brokers

In the USA, business brokers offer a comprehensive and expert service to buyers and sellers. In Europe, including the UK, business brokers tend to offer only an introduction service between buyers and sellers. In some ways, this may be com-pared with the services provided by the traditional estate agent.

It must be understood that the fee basis most business brokers adopt in the UK is 'no deal—no fee'. Even more sig-nificant, they usually expect to receive their fee from the pur-chaser, although they have been appointed by the vendors to sell their business.

This must motivate business brokers to:

▷　encourage people to sell their business rather than pursue other options

▷　complete a deal at the offered price, even though it may be possible to do better

It should not be assumed that business brokers are experts in valuation, taxation or negotiation. Positive proof is required. It is uncommon for business brokers to be involved in the negotiation at all. Most business brokers assume the stance of the nice guy in the middle 'who does not take sides'. Fur-thermore, prospective purchasers have a marked tendency not to want business brokers present during the negotiations. In one instance where the broker suggested negotiating on behalf of the vendors, the prospective purchaser said 'I am happy to pay your scale fee for a completed deal but I will *not* have you present to act against me'.

The 'no deal—no fee' approach may make brokers look attractive, but some of them gossip. They are keen to tell as many people as possible which businesses they are selling, not only to find purchasers for a particular company but to convince people that they have a large number of businesses for sale at any time. Gossip can damage a company which is for sale if the information travels back to either employees or customers. Strict confidentiality must be expected and demanded of any adviser connected with a disposal, and business brokers should be reminded of this.

Merchant and investment banks

The leading European and US banks, who are active in acquisitions and disposal work, undoubtably have demonstrable ability to handle takeover bids for stock market listed companies, whether acting for the bidder or the defender. Equally, they are likely to have considerable experience of handling the disposal of substantial subsidiaries for major groups, using the auction route if appropriate.

For the disposal of a privately owned and often much smaller company, a major bank may be an unsuitable choice of adviser for several reasons. The banks may have relatively little experience of this type of deal, because they prefer to handle larger deals which offer much higher rewards for themselves. Furthermore, some leading banks have a minimum deal fee they expect to obtain which may make them positively expensive for deals under £5 million in value.

What is more, some banks show a marked reluctance to become involved with negotiations. When acting for purchasers, for example, they seem to favour a written offer without any preliminary negotiation. The real danger of this approach is that it risks losing a deal because the other issues which are of real concern to the vendors have not been addressed.

When choosing advisers the maxim of 'horses for courses'

should be applied. Particularly for the disposal of a private company, it is important to establish that the bank:

▷ has experience of similar vendors

▷ welcomes acting for this type of client, especially as it cannot lead to a long-term relationship

▷ offers an acceptable fee level, both for a completed deal and for abortive work if no deal results

Acquisition and disposal specialists

Both in Europe and the USA, a number of relatively small acquisition and disposal specialists have been formed during the last twenty years. Sometimes these companies are referred to as 'corporate finance boutiques', presumably reflecting their modest size.

Livingstone Fisher Associates, based in London, was formed in 1976 by Barrie Pearson and is typical of the most successful and highly respected acquisition and disposal specialists.

Leading acquisition and disposal specialists act for buyers and sellers ranging from major multinationals to privately owned companies. It is likely that their work primarily involves the purchase and sale of private companies and subsidiaries, because most of them lack the market-making capability and capital resources offered by banks. Most of their deals are likely to range in value between £1 million and £50 million, although some deals will be much larger.

Acquisition and disposal specialists attempt to offer as close to one-stop shopping for acquisition and disposal work as possible. Their services are likely to include:

▷ strategic advice on the other options available and help to pursue them

▷ objective guidance on preparing for and timing a sale

▷ writing the description of the business for prospective purchasers

▷ valuing the business

▷ identifying and approaching prospective purchasers from home and overseas

▷ providing or arranging the tax expertise required

▷ managing the auction process if appropriate

▷ leading the negotiation

▷ recommending an individual partner in a particular law firm to handle the legal work, if requested

▷ nursing the deal to legal completion

A particular bank, chartered accountant or law firm may not be a suitable choice as professional adviser because of a lack of particularly relevant experience, but one can assume they are reputable. In contrast, some acquisition and disposal specialists may be cowboys. Positive proof of their clients, track record and professionalism is required.

How to pick advisers

It should be relatively easy to decide the type of adviser to choose, as outlined already in this chapter, based upon the range of expertise required and the size and complexity of the deal.

The real problem is how to pick a particular adviser of a given type. The tried and trusted method of asking acquaintances for suggestions is an obvious starting point.

The financial sections of national newspapers and in some cases, the relevant trade press will mention the names of advisers in reports of completed acquisitions and disposals.

Specialist magazines can be particularly helpful. In the UK, *Acquisitions Monthly* is devoted entirely to acquisitions and disposals, as the name suggests. It contains informative articles by leading advisers, profiles of particular banks and specialist advisers, and details of completed acquisitions and the advisers involved.

If it has been decided that the existing chartered accountants or lawyers used by the company are not sufficiently experienced to handle the disposal, they may at least be able to make enquiries to suggest possible advisers.

Regardless of their reputation, and the strength of the recommendation to use them, any prospective advisers should be expected to provide the following information:

▷ particular services offered

▷ any experience within the same industry sector and of similar sized deals

▷ a list of recent clients

▷ details of deals completed recently

▷ disposal assignments which did not result in a sale, and the reasons

▷ two or three relevant clients to telephone

▷ the people who will do the work and their experience

▷ their approach to ensuring confidentiality

▷ specific advisers they have faced on the other side

▷ the basis of fees if successful and, most importantly, if no deal results

▷ their approach to handling this particular disposal

There are several sales pitches to be rejected, including:

▷ the high valuation come-on—an unrealistically high, and probably unobtainable, valuation is put forward in order to win the assignment. Surprisingly, people do fall for this sales pitch

▷ the switch sell—the initial contact is with a truly impressive director, who is an expert salesperson and probably capable of doing a first-class job. Unfortunately, the work is then switched to an inexperienced person who was not even present at the first meeting

▷ vagueness on fees—it is essential to know at the outset, and have confirmed in writing, the services to be provided and the fees payable. Clarity is essential. Time fees should state hourly rates. Either a budgetary estimate should be provided or a fee limit agreed if no deal results. If a scale fee is to apply for a completed deal, the detail must be set out and it should be clear whether it is to be paid by the purchaser or the vendor. Some advisers deliberately do not mention fees at all, unless the prospective client raises the subject. The advice is unequivocal. *Always* clarify fees at the initial meeting with prospective advisers

When to appoint advisers

To get the most benefit, without necessarily increasing the costs involved, outside advisers should be appointed when the various options available are being evaluated. The reaction of many disposal clients is 'advisers would say that wouldn't they'.

There are several positive reasons for appointing advisers sufficiently early:

▷ the feasibility, benefits, disadvantages and costs of various options must be evaluated on the merits of the particular case

▷ timing is of the essence, and if it is premature to sell now then it is better to know this before having negotiations with a prospective purchaser only to find out that the purchase price offered is almost certain to be unacceptably low

▷ some vendors simply do not realise the potential value of their business as a result of having become a leader in an attractive niche market—they may provide a major company with the opportunity for rapid international expansion of the business or simply have substantial rarity value arising from a lack of similar attractive companies available to buy

Equally importantly, there are several pitfalls which should be avoided by appointing advisers early:

▷ reaching verbal agreement with one purchaser, as a result of an unsolicited approach, without evaluating and approaching other prospective purchasers at home and overseas before any negotiations commence

▷ believing a deal has been done, subject to contract, merely by agreeing a price. In one instance, the vendors agreed a price with a listed company on their undisclosed assumption that one freehold property and a subsidiary company had been excluded. It seemed entirely logical to them because the particular freehold property was owned by them as individuals and they had never intended to sell the subsidiary. The purchasers had assumed that both the property and the subsidiary were included because no indication to the contrary had been given. It was not a negotiation ploy by a purchaser, but a real failure to define what was being sold

▷ reaching agreement on an earn-out deal without realising the unfavourable capital gains tax consequences or defining adequately the method of calculating profits on which the earn-out payments are to be based

▷ having allowed a comprehensive on-site investigation by external accountants, in one case taking six weeks, before negotiating a deal or, worse still, even establishing a price range. It is somewhat inevitable that staff will deduce the business is being sold during an accountancy investigation, despite strenuous efforts or subterfuge to prevent it. Furthermore, commercially sensitive information will have been given prematurely and considerable management time spent in providing information, perhaps abortively

▷ reaching agreement without knowing which company is to be the purchaser, or whether a known purchaser has the ability to pay for the company. This may seem staggering, even unthinkable. It does happen and more frequently than vendors may like to believe it does. In one case, the vendors reached agreement with two directors of a listed company only to be told that an off-the-shelf company to be formed by the two directors would buy the business and sell off one part before selling the remainder to the listed company. Another example was an offer made of over £4 million cash by a company which was discovered to have a balance sheet worth of less than £10,000 as a result of a routine check by the advisers. The truth was that the purchaser had omitted to say that it was the intention to find an institution to finance the purchase

THE COST OF DISPOSAL ADVICE

Chartered accountants and lawyers

Chartered accountants and law firms usually charge on a time basis. Large firms based in major cities are likely to charge substantially more than a small local firm. The cost of a senior partner in one of the largest firms may be up to about £400 per hour for acquisition and disposal work. So it is essential to obtain a budgetary estimate or maximum fee limit at the outset.

Business brokers

Business brokers usually work on a 'no deal—no fee' basis and on completion their fee is calculated on a set scale. A widely used fee scale is:

5 per cent of the first £1 million
plus 4 per cent of the second £1 million
plus 3 per cent of the third £1 million
plus 2 per cent of the fourth £1 million
plus 1 per cent of the balance

This means that the introduction fee on a completed sale ranges from £90,000 on a £2 million deal to £200,000 on a £10 million deal.

Some people bitterly object to the level of the fee for merely providing an introduction, and perhaps this is understandable. On the other hand, the majority of business brokers probably complete only one or two deals per fee earner each year, and the typical deal is likely to be small. So the profits tend not to be exceptionally large.

Merchant and investment banks

There is a tendency by banks to charge fees for acquisition and disposal work based on their assessment of added value to the client. Somewhat cynical business people have expressed the view that this is merely to justify a blank cheque approach to fee levels.

Some of the larger banks have minimum deal fees of at least £100,000, which are not readily disclosed, to avoid smaller and less profitable deals. Provided the minimum fee is exceeded, a bank may charge in the region of 2 to $2\frac{1}{2}$ per cent for a completed deal. It is essential, however, to know the maximum fee or at least the basis of fee calculation if no deal results.

Acquisition and disposal specialists

If advice and help is needed from acquisition and disposal specialists simply to advise and negotiate a sale with one particular purchaser, then a percentage fee on completion should be rejected and a fee agreed based on the time spent.

Frequently, however, acquisition and disposal specialists will be involved from the outset. They usually charge on a scale fee for a completed deal, and one scale which is used is known as the Livingstone Fisher Scale:

$2\frac{1}{2}$ per cent of the first £2 million
plus $1\frac{1}{2}$ per cent of the second £2 million
plus 1 per cent on the balance

This gives a fee of £50,000 for a £2 million deal and £140,000 for a £10 million deal. These fee levels are almost certainly lower than a business broker or a leading bank would charge, although it must be remembered that unlike banks and disposal specialists, business brokers usually work on a 'no deal—no fee' basis. So it is essential to agree an acceptable basis and maximum charge with an acquisition and disposal specialist if no deal results. A relatively low maximum fee limit should be negotiated in the event that no deal is completed, so that the specialist company do not make a profit unless a deal is completed.

HOW TO GET THE BEST FROM ADVISERS

An effective and enjoyable relationship with disposal advisers depends upon:

▷ chemistry

▷ style

▷ availability

Chemistry

It is important not merely to choose advisers by their reputation but to be satisfied that a rapport exists between the individuals concerned. Teamwork and trust are essential ingredients for effective advice and help.

Style

Some advisers are pompous and arrogant, unnecessarily so. Others are technically pedantic and seemingly uncommercial in their approach. A few are used to dealing only with experienced acquirers, rather than vendors who are probably selling a business for the first time, and visibly dislike explaining their advice or being asked to give their reasons. Question any prospective advisers to find out their approach and degree of flexibility before appointing them.

Availability

It can be frustrating when an adviser seems never to be available to receive a telephone call and tardy in telephoning back. It is desirable that at least two people are involved in the advisory team, not only to provide reasonable availability, but also to ensure continuity despite holidays or unexpected illness.

EXECUTIVE SUMMARY

▷ Decide the tasks to be done which require, or would benefit from, outside advice and help

▷ Consider existing advisers before approaching different ones

▷ Choose 'horses for courses' when deciding which type of adviser to use. Consider the suitability of chartered accountants, lawyers, business brokers, merchant and investment banks, and acquisition and disposal specialists

▷ Ask penetrating questions to assess their ability, integrity and professionalism

▷ Ensure fees are confirmed in writing at the outset, covering both a completed deal and the maximum amount payable for abortive work if no deal results

▷ Appoint advisers at the outset for them to deliver the best value for money

▷ Ensure that some sort of 'chemistry' exists and that the advisers' business style is appropriate

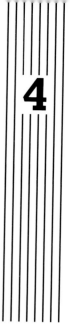

How to Prepare a Company for Sale

Houses need preparing for sale in order to obtain the best price, and so do companies.

When selling a home, a modest amount spent on redecoration and minor repairs makes the place look more attractive and cared for. When selling a company, the preparation must be much more than a few superficial cosmetic improvements.

The preparatory work involved in selling a company can be categorised as follows:

▷ essential preliminaries

▷ deciding what to sell

▷ good housekeeping

▷ separating out a subsidiary or division

▷ enhancing value for the shareholders

Each of these categories will be described in detail.

ESSENTIAL PRELIMINARIES

Circumstances which are likely to dissuade prospective purchasers from buying the company need to be resolved before it is offered for sale. It is naïve to think that a purchaser will not discover them during the 'due diligence' investigation work prior to legal completion. Worse still, by then significant cost will have been incurred and the staff may be unsettled by rumours that the company is being sold.

Potential barriers to a sale include:

▷ litigation

▷ warranty claims

▷ problems with the Inland Revenue

▷ planning uncertainties affecting land and property

▷ compliance requirements of regulatory bodies

▷ legislation affecting product specifications

In general, the likelihood, threat or even possibility of one of these situations arising, and the consequent uncertainty, is more off-putting to a prospective purchaser than if the full extent of the problem is known.

Each of these potential barriers will be considered in turn.

Litigation

Probably the majority of companies are involved in or faced with the possibility of some kind of routine litigation at any time. Examples include the pursuit of monies owed to or by the company, and perhaps an unfair dismissal case. These are unlikely to prove to be a barrier to the sale of the business.

Litigation which could be commercially damaging or expensive to resolve may well prove a hazard. One actual case involved a building products company which had recently entered the US market. An American company wrote to say that the company's major product infringed their patents and that they would take vigorous action to stop further sales in the

USA. A dispute of this kind may take years to resolve and may well render the company temporarily unsaleable.

Warranty claims

If a new product has been launched on a large scale and serious design or manufacturing faults have been discovered, then there could be substantial warranty claims to be faced in the months ahead. Fortunately, in such a case, it should be possible to estimate fairly accurately the anticipated warranty costs in excess of the standard provisions included in the accounts and to demonstrate that the fault has already been eliminated in subsequent production.

Tax problems

An investigation in progress by the Inland Revenue, or the threat of one arising in the light of preliminary enquiries, understandably unsettles a prospective purchaser. It is far too glib to assume that because the vendors will be required to give comprehensive warranties and indemnities concerning taxation, the problem need not concern prospective acquirers. Purchasers are well aware of the professional cost and management time involved in handling an Inland Revenue investigation, and are likely to be concerned that other problems may be raised by them.

Issues which may cause serious tax problems include such mundane matters as benefits in kind for directors and senior staff, and the payment of people on a self-employed basis when they should have been treated as employees.

The only possible advice to anyone envisaging selling a company at any time in the future is to handle all the tax affairs impeccably from the outset.

Planning uncertainties

Planning uncertainties affecting land and buildings can be either negative or positive, but both may affect the sale. A negative uncertainty concerned a freehold building on the outskirts of a major city which had a 'trade counter' and parking for customers along the front. As part of the 'due diligence' investigation work, it was discovered that the planning authorities had prepared a provisional scheme for a motorway spur road to be built which would lead to the loss of the 'trade counter' facilities. Even though it was only a provisional scheme, and other alternatives were being considered by the authorities, the purchaser withdrew from the deal because of the uncertainty involved.

A positive uncertainty concerned the possible opportunity to redevelop a large site, and to relocate the business locally without the loss of key staff. The vendors offered written evidence that planning permission would be obtainable and gave examples of the prices obtained for similar residential development sites in the city. Not surprisingly, prospective purchasers were not prepared to pay a price for the business which reflected the full redevelopment potential value. The vendors were faced with relocating the business first in order to eliminate the uncertainty to a prospective purchaser.

Compliance requirements

From time to time, regulatory bodies are created in a particular country and businesses must be approved by a given date in order to continue trading. Recent examples have affected financial services companies offering investment products and advice in the UK. If there is any doubt about the ability of a company to meet the regulatory requirements, then this will seriously affect the sale of the business in the meantime.

Product specification legislation

Legislation has been introduced in EEC countries concerning the specification of food products, which has affected manufacturers to varying degrees. Some have needed to make expensive changes to their product specifications or production processes. Clearly, if there is forthcoming legislation affecting the products of a company which is for sale, a prospective purchaser will want to be satisfied that the requirements have been addressed and the impact on the business evaluated.

WHAT TO SELL

Matters which need to be considered, and resolved where appropriate, include:

▷ directors' other interests

▷ the ownership of property used by the business

▷ overseas companies, including dormant ones

Each of these will be considered in turn.

Directors' other interests

A purchaser will need to be satisfied that there will be no conflict of interest after the sale. For example, the directors may be shareholders in a related business, which could compete to some extent with the business to be sold or create confusion amongst customers if a similar trading name is involved. Alternatively, a director may own and have a part-time role in a quite different business. If the purchaser requires the full-time executive involvement of the director in the business to be sold, then this potential conflict will have to be resolved.

In deciding what to include in the sale, the golden rule must be to avoid any possible conflict of interest after the disposal.

Ownership of property

In private companies, it is not unusual for properties used by the business to be owned by the shareholders as individuals, as part of their tax planning. As the company and the property are owned by the same individuals, it is quite normal that neither formal lease nor rental agreement exists for the use of the property by the business. An open mind should be kept whether or not to include the sale of the property with the business.

For example, if the value of the property is likely to increase substantially because it will benefit from planned motorway development, then it may make sense to offer only a short lease to the purchaser of the business.

Decisions made by private companies may make sound sense at the time, but may be a barrier to the sale of the business many years later. In an actual case, a company had the opportunity to buy an attractive retail property in the 1960s. The company could not afford to buy the whole property, even with the help of the largest loan available, so it was decided to buy it jointly between the company and a wealthy shareholder. A commercial rent was paid for the half of the property owned by the individual, and everything was fine. When the business was to be sold over twenty years later in 1987, the purchaser rightly insisted that the property had to be either included or excluded from the sale because a half share in the freehold was unacceptable.

Purchasers tend to become nervous when overseas property is involved. They will want satisfactory evidence that the title is owned by the company. If this cannot be established, then it could affect the sale of the business. It must make sense whenever buying property overseas to ensure that the legal work is handled professionally and that adequate evidence of title is available.

Overseas companies

Some companies register overseas subsidiaries in order to protect the use of the company name. Perhaps some of the subsidiaries do actually trade. It may seem attractive to a vendor not to sell these because it may provide an opportunity to establish overseas residency for tax purposes and to have a continuing business interest as well. It must be recognised, however, that a prospective purchaser will wish to avoid any conflict or the inability to use a valuable trading name in another country.

GOOD HOUSEKEEPING

The lack of good housekeeping is unlikely to present a barrier to the sale of a company, but it may cause some delay. The existence of it, however, is an indication of professional management and is likely to be reassuring to a purchaser.

The elements of good housekeeping include:

▷   shareholder agreement to sell

▷   share structure

▷   taxation affairs

▷   accountancy policies

▷   employment contracts

▷   incentive schemes

▷   intellectual property

Each of these will be considered in turn.

Shareholder agreement to sell

A purchaser will usually wish to be satisfied that 100 per cent of the equity is available to purchase, even in an earn-out deal. Alternatively, if only a tranche of the equity is to be purchased initially, the purchaser may insist on an option to purchase the remainder. So it is essential to obtain the agreement of all the shareholders to sell their shares. If some of the shares are owned by a financial institution they may only agree provided that a given price can be obtained, and one which may not be at all easy to achieve. If some of the equity is held in a trust, then extra time may be needed to obtain the requisite agreement to sell. If one of the shareholders has died without leaving a will, or probate of a will has not been granted, this may cause delay.

It is a necessary preliminary step to obtain the agreement of all the shareholders to the sale of the company.

Share structure

The best share structure to have for the sale of a company is simply one class of ordinary shares. Whenever there are different classes of ordinary shares, with different rights attached, or complications such as preference shares or convertible loanstock, there is a risk of disagreement. The different classes of shareholders are likely to have conflicting views concerning the relative values of each class.

So it is desirable at least to reach some agreement about relative values before the company is offered for sale, and anything which is done to simplify the share structure helps to avoid disagreements at the negotiation stage.

Taxation affairs

Purchasers are reassured when all the taxation affairs of the company are up to date, in correct order, and the approval of the Inland Revenue has been obtained for computations submitted.

This applies to all tax affairs including:

▷ corporation tax

▷ capital gains tax

▷ employee income tax

▷ overseas profits and income

> ▷ dividends received and paid

> ▷ benefits in kind for directors and senior staff

There is merit in always ensuring that all tax affairs are kept up to date continuously, but perhaps this is a counsel of perfection. One thing is certain, however: as soon as a decision to sell the business has been taken then strenuous efforts should be made to bring the tax affairs up to date.

Accounting policies

It must be realised that as soon as the sale of a company is legally completed, a purchaser will install common accounting policies. Furthermore, it is completely naïve to assume that a purchaser will be fooled by accountancy policies which artificially inflate profits, for example the use of extended periods for the depreciation of fixed assets. Purchasers usually restate the profits of the target company using their own accounting policies as part of their valuation calculations. So there is no benefit to be gained by choosing accounting policies to artificially inflate profits.

Employment contracts

In many countries, legislation requires that each employee has a written contract of employment. Some privately owned companies ignore this requirement but it should be complied with as part of their preparation for a sale of the company.

Incentive schemes

Some private companies have individual incentive schemes for directors and senior staff which may be totally unacceptable to a large purchaser. In an electronics company employing about one thousand people, the twelve most senior people had personal incentive schemes which they had negotiated with the principal shareholder and chairperson. Furthermore, the schemes were open-ended and ill thought-out. For example, the group marketing director received a bonus calculated as a fraction of one per cent of total sales, payable even if the company made a loss. Also, no provision had been made to exclude sales resulting from the acquisition of another company. The purchaser insisted that these incentive schemes were 'bought out' prior to legal completion.

Intellectual property

The administration of intellectual property such as patents should be in order and up to date. Patent renewal deadlines should have been met so that adequate patent protection exists. Wherever appropriate, patents should have been applied for in those overseas countries where trading takes place.

SEPARATING OUT A SUBSIDIARY OR DIVISION

Several months may be needed to arrange the affairs of a subsidiary or division so that it can be separated out easily and cleanly.

The issues which need to be addressed include:

▷   premises

▷   use of central services

▷   pension entitlement

▷   use of intellectual property

Each of these will be described in turn.

Premises

There may be various situations which need action. The premises may be owned by a property subsidiary of the group and leased to the business to be sold. A decision must be made whether to not to sell the premises, taking into account the potential increase in value in the foreseeable future and the crystallisation of any capital gains tax liabilities by selling now. Another possibility is that the business to be sold shares the premises with another subsidiary which is to be retained. The use of the space may make it extremely difficult to separate the two businesses effectively. It may be preferable to offer the business for sale on condition that it is relocated within, say, twelve months.

Use of central services

Some central services can be transferred more quickly and easily than others when a subsidiary or division is sold. Routine matters such as payroll preparation and pension administration fall into the 'easy' category. A dependence on an integrated information technology capability may well be difficult to transfer quickly, especially if the hardware or software used by the purchaser proves to be incompatible.

It is unrealistic to think that the information technology issues can be resolved until a particular purchaser is in sight. The preparation which should be done before then, however, is consideration of a reasonable handover period and a basis of charges for services provided in the meantime.

Pension entitlement

The pension fund assets and liabilities relating to those staff who are to be transferred on the sale of the business need to be calculated by a firm of actuaries, or by an insurance company if they manage the group scheme. This is likely to take quite a while and instructions should be given sufficiently early to ensure that legal completion is not delayed.

Use of intellectual property

There may be certain patents, brand names, copyright and other intellectual property owned by the group, which will need to be transferred. This should be relatively routine but a complication may arise if the intellectual property is also used for the benefit of other subsidiaries which are to be retained by the group. Some form of licence will need to be drawn up.

ENHANCING SHAREHOLDER VALUE

The most important preparation work to be done is that designed to increase the financial benefit to the shareholders.

Amongst the aspects of the business requiring adequate preparation prior to disposal are:

▷ full asset valuation

▷ full profit declaration

▷ evidence of rising sales and profits

▷ a strategic plan for the business

▷ effective management information

▷ directors' pensions

▷ a pre-completion dividend

▷ future salaries for directors

Full asset valuation

Properties may not have been revalued for several years. The potential value which could result from residential or retail development of the site must be assessed. In any event, an up-to-date valuation should be obtained.

An existing lease may be on such attractive terms until the next review date, which may be several years away, that a significant premium value exists.

Full profit declaration

Stock and work-in-progress may be valued conservatively by private companies in order to minimise the corporation tax payable. One method is to provide generous stock provisions in the accounts. This has particular significance for the value

to be obtained by shareholders, because an important deter-
minant of the price to be paid for a business is the profit after
tax of the business.

A simplified example will illustrate the significance.
Assume that stock and work-in-progress is undervalued on the
balance sheet at the time of sale by, say, £300,000. If this is
merely pointed out to the purchaser it will have little or no
impact on the price offered. The benefit is likely to be treated
merely as increasing the net asset backing as a percentage of
the purchase price.

Now consider if the £300,000 were to be released into the
profit and loss account during the previous financial year, the
current year and the next one. This would increase the annual
pre-tax profit by £100,000. If the corporation tax rate is 35 per
cent, the increase in profit after tax will be £65,000. If the
purchase price were calculated on, say, ten times post-tax
profit, this would increase the value of the business by £650,000.

As a result of a fall in inflation rates, an actuarial review of
the pension fund may show that the level of company contribution can be reduced. Justifiable opportunities such as this
to reduce costs should be taken.

The message is clear. Do not understate profits in the lead-
up to the sale of a business.

Evidence of rising sales and profits

The natural concern of any purchaser is the risk of buying a
business which has reached a plateau, or worse still, is about
to decline.

The desirable pattern to demonstrate is:

▷ worthwhile sales and profit growth during the
previous three years

▷ a further improvement in prospects for the current
financial year

▷ evidence of another increase during the following
year as a result of business development already in the

pipeline, such as new products, branch openings or overseas expansion

▷ profit margins being maintained or improved

So it is important to strike a balance between the development and profitability of the business in the two or three years prior to the sale.

Strategic plan

When a group is disposing of a business, prospective purchasers will be keen to read the current strategic plan. Whilst projected sales and profit forecasts may be viewed with considerable scepticism, the narrative describing opportunities and business development projects to be pursued will be read with considerable interest.

Relatively few privately owned companies take the trouble to produce a written strategic plan. If one exists, however, it will be looked on favourably by prospective purchasers. If not, the vendors and their professional advisers must adequately describe and sell the business development opportunities to prospective purchasers.

Effective management information

A well-managed business, either privately owned or part of a listed group, should have annual budgets, reliable monthly management accounts produced promptly, and current financial year forecasts of sales and profits updated regularly. Mere opinion of the likely sales and profits for the current financial year is likely to be viewed with scepticism.

The production of budgets, prompt monthly accounts and updated year-end forecasts is sound business. So it makes sense to introduce these well before a sale is intended.

Directors' pensions

In the two or three years prior to a sale, or at least during the year of sale, consideration should be given to the benefit for directors of the company making substantial lump-sum payments to a personal pension scheme, especially if the directors have not made adequate pension arrangements for themselves. From a purchase price standpoint, there should be little or no adverse impact because a purchaser is likely to 'add back' the pension payments as these could not be a continuing cost.

Pre-completion dividend

In some countries, provided the purchaser agrees, it is more tax effective for the vendors to receive a substantial dividend payment before legal completion in exchange for a reduced purchase price. Expert tax advice is essential to evaluate and carry out such an arrangement to avoid tax complications later.

Future salaries for directors

If an earn-out deal is involved, the directors will be keen to keep their salaries low where there is a benefit to be gained under the agreed formula. For example, if the earn-out payments are to be five times the profit before tax over a target figure in the current and following finance year, the lower the directors salaries are set the more they stand to gain from the earn-out payment.

If an outright sale takes place, however, then it is in the directors' interests to negotiate the best possible reward package if they are required to enter into a service contract to manage the business for a period for the new owners. It may be possible to negotiate a profit-related bonus in addition to the basic salary to be paid.

EXECUTIVE SUMMARY

Preparatory work falls into several categories:

▷ some problems, or even potential problems, need to be resolved prior to sale. They include:

- litigation
- warranty claims
- investigation by the Inland Revenue
- compliance requirements of regulatory bodies
- planning uncertainties affecting land and property
- legislation affecting product specification

▷ what is to be sold needs to be decided, including:

- directors' other interests
- ownership of property used by the business
- overseas subsidiaries

▷ good housekeeping which needs to be done before selling includes:

- all the shareholders agreeing to the sale
- relative values of different classes of shares agreed
- taxation affairs and computations agreed and up to date

▷ separating out a subsidiary or division requires:

- sale or lease of property to be decided
- transfer of central services to be considered, especially computerisation
- calculation of pension fund assets and liabilities for staff to be transferred
- transfer or use of intellectual property to be arranged

▷ enhancing shareholder values should involve:

- full asset valuation
- full profit declaration
- evidence of rising sales and profits
- directors' pension arrangements
- a pre-completion dividend, where this is tax-effective

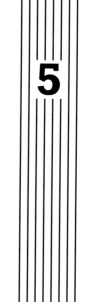

5

How to Handle Approaches

Prospective vendors have a marked tendency to act first and think later when receiving an unsolicited approach or making one themselves. In both cases, careful thought is essential.

Unsolicited approaches fall into two categories:

▷ approach by an intermediary

▷ direct approach by a prospective purchaser

Each of these situations will be considered separately.

APPROACH BY AN INTERMEDIARY

An approach may be received from:

▷ a merchant or investment bank

▷ a firm of chartered accountants

▷ acquisition and disposal specialists

▷ a business broker

It is assumed that either a bank or a firm of chartered accountants will be acting on behalf of a specific client. Reputable acquisition and disposal specialists should make it clear whether they are acting for a specific client or are seeking to be appointed to act for prospective vendors. Some business brokers may give the impression that they are acting for a specific purchaser, when in reality they are simply seeking businesses to sell. In each case, caution is appropriate.

The approach may be made either by letter or telephone, and each requires a different response.

An approach by letter

If there is a definite intention not to sell the business in the foreseeable future, one course of action is simply to throw the letter in the waste-paper bin. Another would be to file it in a deep drawer.

None the less, curiosity may come into play. There may be a desire to find out who wishes to buy the company or what the business might be worth.

If so, the response should depend on whether or not the approach was made by a well-known company. If not, the first thing to ask for is a written list of the deals they have completed in the previous twelve months.

Their business address may give some indication about them. An address which is a street in a small town suggests a 'one man band' operating from home. An unlimited company in the UK suggests a small business. Cowboys do exist. It is essential to be satisfied that the intermediary is a reputable company.

The next step should be to establish by a telephone call:

▷ the name of their client company

▷ the individual in that company they are working for

▷ if the client asked them to make specific approaches

▷ if not, why the particular company was selected for an approach

▷ what basis of reward the intermediary is working on

The answers to the above questions, or lack of them, will give a clear indication of whether it is a carefully targeted approach on behalf of a specific client or merely a general approach within the business sector to find companies to sell. At this stage, it should be made clear that the business is definitely not for sale.

It is quite possible, and reasonable too, that the intermediary is only prepared to name the client at a meeting. This could well be at the request of the client to avoid disclosing their acquisition intentions unless some degree of interest, rather than curiosity, is shown. If a meeting is to take place, then a visit to the intermediary is recommended.

An approach by telephone

Telephone approaches are becoming more commonplace. If the name of the intermediary company is not a familiar one, it may be appropriate to ask for the approach to be made in writing, together with a list of deals completed during the previous twelve months. Then pursue it as described already for dealing with a written approach.

If there is a definite intention not to sell, however, then it is best to end the telephone conversation as soon as possible.

Meeting an intermediary

A meeting with an intermediary, as a result of an unsolicited approach enquiring if the company is available to purchase, should only take place provided that:

▷ the name of the prospective purchaser has been given, or

▷ it will be given at the beginning of the meeting

The approach during the meeting should be to disclose the minimum of information about the company, and to find out as much as possible about the prospective purchaser and the intermediary. At the end of the meeting, it should be made clear either that the company is not for sale or that further thought may be given to the approach, whichever is appropriate.

If there is any wish to pursue a sale, then the next step should be to appoint advisers to provide expert guidance.

DIRECT APPROACH BY A PROSPECTIVE PURCHASER

The approach may be made by a person already known to the directors. Alternatively, it could be by telephone or letter from an unfamiliar company.

Even if the approach is from someone already known, the response should be either a reluctance to sell or a statement that the company is definitely not for sale. Information about the business should be given sparingly.

If the approach is from an unfamiliar company, the first step should be to check that it is a company listed on a stock market. If not, a credit status check will establish, at the cost of a few pounds, the size and purchasing power of the company.

Another type of approach, but a much less frequent one, is from individuals wishing to pursue a management buy-in. This requires a cautious approach. It is reasonable to ask for written details of:

▷   their career to date

▷   the amount of their own money available

▷   evidence of the willingness of a financial institution to back them

Unless this information is convincing, then a meeting should not take place.

An approach may be made seeking a management buy-out. The natural reaction may be a sympathetic one, even a desire to pursue it. However, in order to get an attractive deal, other prospective purchasers must be involved as well.

Meeting a prospective purchaser

Resist any suggestion that the prospective purchaser should visit the company for an initial meeting. Someone, perhaps even the receptionist, may speculate and gossip that the company is to be sold. Remote though this possibility may be, it is a risk to be avoided. The meeting should take place either at the offices of the prospective purchaser or on neutral ground, such as a restaurant, provided that confidentiality is assured.

Once again, the posture should be one of reluctance or curiosity. Little information should be provided. The aim should be to find out the intentions of the prospective purchaser.

The information to be obtained includes:

▷ the authority of the individual making the approach

▷ what higher level of approval is needed before a specific deal can be negotiated

▷ the commercial rationale underlying the approach

▷ which other companies are being approached

▷ how much they know about each company approached

▷ how they intend to expand or rationalise a company acquired

▷ whether an outright purchase or earn-out deal is envisaged

▷ what management continuity they want

▷ the criteria used to decide how much to pay for a company

▷ what timescale to complete a deal is envisaged

This information will give a valuable insight into the importance and urgency of their acquisition plans. The questions need to be asked in a low-key way, however, in order to avoid giving the impression of a willingness to sell.

It may well be suggested that the next step is to visit the company. This should be firmly, and politely, resisted.

If the approach has triggered a desire to explore a sale, the next steps should be to establish that:

▷ a sale is the preferred option

▷ it makes sense to sell now

▷ other prospective purchasers should be involved quickly

Some vendors wait until they are ready to have final negotiations with the company which approached them before appointing advisers. This cannot make sense.

Several weeks will be required to approach other prospective purchasers and progress to the stage where other companies are ready to negotiate. In the meantime, there may be considerable pressure from the company which made the approach either to negotiate a deal or to terminate the discussion.

BEFORE MAKING AN APPROACH TO PROSPECTIVE PURCHASERS

To avoid a waste of management time and the risk of gossip damaging the business, no approach should be made until it has been established that it makes sense to sell the business now, and:

▷ a valuation of the business has been done

▷ a minimum acceptable price has been decided

▷ an asking price has been assessed

▷ prospective purchasers at home and from overseas have been identified

EXECUTIVE SUMMARY

Unsolicited approaches include:

▷ a letter from an intermediary:
  - if no intention to sell, do not pursue
  - be satisfied it is a reputable company
  - confirm it is acting for a specific client
  - arrange any meeting on their premises

▷ a telephone call from an intermediary:
  - ask for written confirmation before considering it

▷ a prospective purchaser making direct contact:
  - from a known person—be guarded
  - from an unfamiliar company—check their financial status
  - a buy-in team—check their credentials and financial backing
  - a buy-out team—request time to consider it

Meet a prospective purchaser on neutral ground and ask penetrating questions

Before making an approach to a prospective purchaser:

▷ decide it makes sense to sell now

▷ carry out a valuation

▷ decide the minimum price acceptable

▷ identify prospective purchasers at home and from overseas

How to Value a Business for Sale

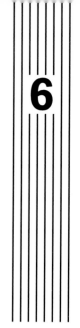

There is no right answer to the value of an unquoted company, whether it is privately owned or a subsidiary of a group, and it can even be argued that the only meaningful valuation is the highest amount which a prospective purchaser is willing to pay.

None the less, it is possible in most cases to calculate the likely price range which can be achieved with an acceptable degree of accuracy.

For owners of private companies, it is not enough simply to assess the likely purchase price of the business. The amount to be obtained by an executive director, after paying capital gains tax, may not be sufficient to finance early retirement. Yet for a person of, say, forty-five, it may be difficult or simply unattractive to make a new career. So the loss of annual income needs to be weighed carefully against the capital sum to be obtained.

Executive directors of private companies are not in the habit of calculating the annual cost of sustaining their present life style out of capital. Yet the calculation must be made.

Consider someone aged forty-five, who enjoys a lifestyle which costs £60,000 a year as an executive director. Assume the sale of the company would require retirement from the business after one year. If the amount to be received for the individual shareholding was £500,000, this would be reduced to little more than £300,000 after paying capital gains tax in the UK. Clearly this amount would not sustain the existing lifestyle to normal retirement age. Also, the pension to follow would be reduced substantially because of the premature termination of pension contributions.

People tend to underestimate the cost of maintaining a lifestyle enjoyed by the executive directors of a private company. In addition to salary, other benefits to take into account include:

> the provision of a car and all motoring expenses

> another car which may be provided for a spouse

> any dividends received

> opportunities for combining business with pleasure, such as foreign travel and eating out

> pension contributions paid by the company

> any other fringe benefits

It is not unusual for the total cost of these items to exceed the salary received.

THE FUNDAMENTALS OF VALUING A BUSINESS

The price any purchaser is prepared to pay is likely to be determined by the profit and cash flow produced from owning the business, and to a lesser degree by the balance sheet worth of the assets.

The importance of adjusted profits

Purchasers of businesses usually produce adjusted profit figures for at least the previous financial year, the current one, and several years into the future.

To value a business on behalf of vendors requires a similar

approach, and the professional advisers are likely to present adjusted profit figures to prospective purchasers.

From the vendor's standpoint it is worth adjusting profits for the previous three to five years if this will help to establish a record of rising profits. One-off events which may have significantly reduced profits in any one year include:

▷ a large bad debt as a result of a major customer going into liquidation

▷ the costs of relocating a factory, warehouse or office

▷ a strike affecting deliveries from a key supplier or sales to a major customer

▷ the costs arising from major litigation

▷ the closure of premises or the termination of a product

▷ the start-up costs associated with entering an overseas market

▷ significant redundancy costs

▷ lump-sum pension contributions for directors

Additionally, there may be factors which will enhance profits for the new owners, such as:

▷ the directors being required to accept a reasonable executive salary after the sale, compared with the substantial rewards enjoyed as owners and directors

▷ the intention that a director will retire upon the sale of the business and will not need to be replaced

▷ the savings arising from the termination of relatives working for the business at inflated salaries

▷ the benefits to be gained from recently taken action such as a price increase, the elimination of a loss making activity, and so on

It is particularly important that the profits for the previous financial year and the current one are adjusted to show the most favourable picture which can be portrayed accurately.

In the case of the disposal of a division or subsidiary, it is important to adjust the profits by 'adding back' charges allocated by the present group which will not be made following a disposal. These include a wide range of possible allocated costs such as:

▷ a group management charge based on the cost of a proportion of central staff costs

▷ a percentage levy based on sales value for group expenditure, such as research and development or public relations

▷ service charges for the use of central departments such as information technology, payroll and pension administration, and so on

The reality is that the acquiring company will be able to provide the resources required at a much lower incremental cost than is presently allocated by the existing group. Equally, it must be realised that the overall impact on the profits of the existing group will be significantly larger than the profits reported by the subsidiary. The reason is that in practice it will not be possible to reduce group costs by the amount allocated to the subsidiary. For example, the sale of a subsidiary is unlikely to reduce commensurately the amount which needs to be spent centrally on research and development or public relations.

Equally, if the aim is to make a realistic assessment of the worth of a business to a purchaser, it would be naïve to ignore the extra costs which will be incurred.

Examples of the extra costs which will be taken into account by a prospective purchaser are:

▷ the appointment of a qualified financial controller to replace an unqualified bookkeeper

▷ the need for increased insurance cover

▷ increasing some salaries to avoid unacceptable differentials compared with similar staff already employed within the group

▷ additional pension contributions arising from employees joining the group pension scheme

The acquiring company will take into account opportunities for increased profits as a result of acquiring the business. It is equally important that these are quantified by the vendor as well. Typical opportunities to increase profits are:

▷ purchase cost savings as a result of increased purchasing power

▷ cross selling the products and services of the acquired company to existing group customers, and vice versa, both at home and overseas

▷ the rationalisation of premises and overhead costs

The aim must be to negotiate a purchase price which reflects a share of the profit opportunities arising from the acquisition being enjoyed by the vendors.

Cash flow projections

Purchasers will be concerned to make detailed cash flow projections, probably for at least three years forward, as part of the valuation exercise. Vendors should prepare at least outline cash flow projections as an important part of their own valuation.

Factors which need to be taken into account include:

▷ the amount of cash to be generated, or injection needed, based on the expected business growth

▷ the need for capital expenditure to replace existing assets or to refurbish premises

▷ capital expenditure to meet the planned expansion

▷ the cash proceeds arising from the sale or redevelopment of surplus assets

▷ cash balances in the balance sheet at present

When acquiring a service company, on an earn-out deal spread over several years, the cost of deferred payments may be generated out of cash retained by the acquired company. If this type of situation is not quantified, the company may be sold at too low a price.

If there is surplus cash in the company, consideration should be given to the possibility of using it for the tax-effective benefit of the owners by making lump-sum pension payments or paying a pre-completion dividend. If the cash is not used in this way before completion, it must be fully reflected in the purchase price.

In a similar way, cash to be generated by the disposal of surplus assets after the sale must be reflected in the purchase price.

Adjusted balance sheet worth

The most recent and audited balance sheet should be adjusted to reflect the current net asset worth by taking into account:

▷ the market value of freehold premises

▷ the premium value attaching to property leases

▷ retained profits since the balance sheet date

It has been explained that understated current assets such as stocks, work-in-progress and debtors should be adjusted through the profit and loss account.

VALUATION CRITERIA AND FACTORS

Adjusted profits, cash flow forecasts and present balance sheet net asset worth need to be calculated rigorously.

It would be wrong to assume, however, that an accurate valuation can be made simply by arithmetic application of financial criteria or formulae. Less quantifiable factors must be taken into account as well.

The financial criteria widely used by purchasers and experienced advisers alike are:

    ▷   an earnings-multiple approach

    ▷   discounted cash flow analysis techniques

    ▷   return on investment

    ▷   impact on earnings per share for a listed company making an acquisition

    ▷   net asset backing

The less easily quantified factors which should be taken into account include:

    ▷   scarcity, rarity or uniqueness value

    ▷   a defensive need to acquire

    ▷   upstream and downstream profit benefits

Each of the above criteria and factors will be explored in detail.

Earnings multiples

An earnings-multiple approach to the valuation of a business means that the purchase price is calculated by:

    ▷   taking the adjusted profit before tax for the previous financial year

    ▷   deducting a full tax charge, calculated at the standard corporation tax rate

    ▷   multiplying the above profit after tax by an appropriate number of years

The application of this method depends upon the appropriate number of years chosen to multiply by the profits after tax, which are often referred to as earnings.

The basis of this method is an attempt to relate the value of unquoted companies to similar companies listed on a stock market in the same country. Stock market listed companies have a price/earnings ratio, often described as a PE Ratio, which is the equivalent of an earnings multiple.

A PE Ratio is calculated as follows:

$$\text{PE Ratio} = \frac{\text{present market share price}}{\text{historical earnings per share}}$$

The historical earnings per share is the profits after tax for the previous financial year divided by the average number of issued shares during that year.

An illustration may be helpful. Assume:

present market share price	= 182p
previous year's profit after tax	= £2.6 million
average number of issued shares that year	= 20.0 million

therefore, earnings per share $= \dfrac{£2.6}{20.0} = 13p$

therefore, PE Ratio $= \dfrac{182p}{13p} = 14.0$

It is accurate to state as a generalisation, however, that an unquoted company would be valued at a lower earnings multiple than the PE Ratio which exists for a listed company carrying out a similar business in the same market sector.

A major reason for this difference can be explained by the fact that there is not a market, and hence no opportunity to buy and sell shares, in the equity of an unquoted company. In the case of a private company, the success of the business may be unduly dependent upon the continued executive involvement and commitment of the present owners during the short to medium term. This will therefore tend to reduce the worth of the business to a prospective purchaser.

Recent empirical evidence shows that the earnings multiples reflected in the prices paid for unquoted companies reveal discounts ranging from 20 to 50 per cent compared to the PE Ratio of a quoted company in the same market sector with similar prospects for the rate of future profit growth. The size of the discount is influenced by the attractiveness of a market sector in tems of future growth and the availability of companies to acquire.

If the company to be sold is suitable to obtain a stock market quotation, and it is ready to float quickly, then a value of the business can be negotiated on the basis of the PE Ratio which would apply on flotation less the total costs of admission to the stock market. Any suggestion of a discount on the comparable PE Ratio should therefore be rejected.

Discounted cash flow analysis techniques

Whole books have been devoted to the application of discounted cash flow analysis techniques, so it will be appreciated that only an outline of the method can be given here.

Discounted cash flow techniques are widely used by sizeable companies for the evaluation of capital expenditure projects. The technique requires the cash flows to be calculated over a period of several years. Therefore, the cash flow elements which need to be quantified are:

> ▷ the initial purchase consideration

> ▷ subsequent earn-out payments

> ▷ the annual operating cash flow from the business taking into account all capital expenditure needs and movements in working capital

> ▷ the realisable value of the assets remaining at the end of the period chosen for the evaluation

> ▷ taxation payments

The discounted cash flow process can be used to evaluate the pattern of cash outflows and inflows to produce different measures of performance. These are:

NET PRESENT VALUE

This is sometimes referred to as NPV, and is the present value of the cash flows calculated at the percentage discount rate set by the company. Provided that the NPV is a positive figure, rather than a negative one, it means that the acquisition is calculated to exceed the rate of return required by the company.

INTERNAL RATE OF RETURN OR % DCF RATE OF RETURN

The rate of return calculation is much more widely used than net present values. The rate of return is found by calculating the discount rate at which the net present value of the cash outflows and inflows equals zero over the evaluation period chosen.

DISCOUNTED PAY BACK PERIOD

The discounted pay back period is the number of years required to generate sufficient cash, discounted usually at a standard rate of 10 per cent, to equal or 'pay back' the initial cash outflow.

Whereas it is not unusual for companies to expect or demand a discounted pay back period not exceeding three years for organic growth projects, the premiums over net asset value paid to acquire companies means that the periods may be considerably longer for acquisition.

Discounted cash flow analysis is extremely relevant conceptually for the evaluation of acquisitions because it focuses entirely on the generation of cash. There are some pitfalls, however, when using the method and it is important to be aware of these.

Companies use lengthy periods for evaluation, ranging from five or seven years to as long as fifteen or twenty years. Obviously, the accuracy of the cash flow projections after the first two or three years must be questionable. Fortunately, the weighting given to cash flows in later years is much less than for the early years because this is inherent in the nature of the calculations.

Within a large group, it is desirable to set a standard number of years over which any acquisition will be evaluated to ensure uniformity of evaluation.

One other subjective issue is the realisable value of the assets remaining at the end of the period of evaluation. When using discounted cash flow techniques to evaluate internal capital expenditure projects, it is usual merely to include the market value of land and buildings and whatever value might be realised for other assets. For consistency of treatment, most companies tend to use a similar approach for acquisition evaluation. This means they do not assume that the business will be sold as a going concern, at a premium over net asset value, at the end of the period.

One of the real benefits of using discounted cash flow techniques is the use of sensitivity analysis to answer 'what if' questions. For example, an advertising agency acquiring a competitor might be rightly concerned at the risk of losing a major account because of a conflict of interest caused by representing two clients in the same business sector. Sensitivity analysis allows another percentage rate of return and discounted pay back period calculation to be made quickly to determine the effect of the loss of a client.

In summary, discounted cash flow techniques are used by some of the more sophisticated acquirers. Even if the discounting is not done, the calculation of annual cash flows alone will give a valuable insight into the benefits to be gained by the acquirer.

Return on investment

By now, readers who are not accountants may be wishing that a simple rule of thumb could be provided.

Well it can. The return on investment is easily calculated. What is more, this simple method is popular with group chief executives of large companies as a way to cut through the complicated financial analysis often carried out by their corporate finance staff.

Return on investment, often abbreviated as ROI, can be defined in various ways. A simple and useful definition is:

$$\text{percentage return on investment} = \frac{\text{pre-tax profit from acquisition}}{\text{cash invested}}$$

A simplified example may be helpful. Consider a civil engineering contracting firm purchased for £2.4 million and earn-out payments of £0.3 million expected to be paid in each of the next two years. Further information is set out below:

	First Year	Second Year	Third Year
Pre-tax profit forecast	£450,000	£550,000	£650,000
Purchase consideration	£(2.4) m	£(0.3)	£(0.3)
Net cash generated	£0.1 m	£0.4	£0.5
Cumulative net cash outlay	£2.3 m	£2.2	£2.0

$$\text{Return on investment} = \frac{£450,000}{£2.3\,m} \quad \frac{£550,000}{£2.2} \quad \frac{£650,000}{£2.0}$$

$$= 19.6\% \quad 25\% \quad 32.5\%$$

Most companies seek to achieve a return of between 20 and 25 per cent on the above basis, but may well recognise that acquisition prices mean that this level may only be achievable during the first or second year following acquisition.

So, expressed in the most simple terms, a business which will enable the acquirer to increase their total profits by, say, £1 million in the second year following acquisition would be valued at between £4 million and £5 million, to give a return on investment of 25 and 20 per cent respectively.

Net asset backing

For a company achieving reasonable profitability, net asset backing will be a secondary factor in determining the price to be paid. In a service company where asset backing is particularly low, such as a firm of insurance brokers, the impact is likely to be an insistence on an earn-out deal.

When a company is making losses or doing only a little better than breaking even, asset backing is likely to have an important effect on the purchase price.

With a loss-making company, the purchase value is likely to be significantly less than the net asset value at the time of negotiating the purchase. Assume the company is making losses at the rate of £500,000 a year, and there will be an interval of, say, six weeks between negotiation and legal completion. This means that the net worth will have diminished by about £60,000 in the meantime, because the losses are roughly £10,000 per week. Furthermore, it is likely to take months rather than weeks to eliminate losses after legal completion, which will further diminish the net asset worth before profits are restored. Also, it has to be said that purchasers are likely to attach only a minimal value to accumulated tax losses to be carried forward.

When selling a loss-making company, the reality often becomes horse trading to negotiate the discount on net asset value rather than carrying out a valuation. A forecast of dramatic profit growth within the next two or three years, despite losses in the previous and current years, will be viewed cautiously by prospective purchasers. Their likely reaction is to offer an initial payment related to present net asset worth, and earn-out payments for the achievement of worthwhile profits in the future.

So the message is clear. Take urgent action to restore profits in loss-making companies before selling them. The impact on the purchase price is likely to be substantial. Yet all too often, groups choose to sell a subsidiary *because* it is making a loss. This is the worst possible time to sell. What is more, the only purchaser may be the management team wishing to pursue a buy-out and so reap the benefits for themselves.

Turning round loss-making companies prior to sale is so important that Chapter 10 is devoted to how to do it!

Impact on earnings per share

Companies listed on a stock market are keen to ensure that significant earnings per share growth is achieved every year.

Earnings per share are the profits after tax earned for the benefit of ordinary shareholders divided by the number of issued shares.

This has two effects on the price a particular listed company is likely to be prepared to pay for acquisitions.

Firstly, there is a psychological resistance for a listed company to pay a higher multiple for an unquoted company in the same sector than the PE Ratio of their own shares. This may seem illogical, and it can be argued so. None the less, it is often a reality. So it must be realised that a company with a low PE Ratio is likely to offer a relatively low price.

Secondly, when the acquisition is significant relative to the size of a listed bidder, and it is being financed by a placing of shares or the issue of convertible loanstock, the company will wish to ensure that the acquisition will not adversely affect their earnings per share growth throughout the medium term.

Scarcity, rarity and uniqueness value

There is considerable evidence to demonstrate that purchasers are prepared to pay more than a financial evaluation alone would indicate when there is a scarcity of suitable companies available in a given sector.

Scarcity becomes rarity, which commands a better price still, when there is only one sizeable company left to purchase in a sector within a country. A recent example in the UK was the purchase of the last remaining do-it-yourself retail superstore chain which was still privately owned. By then, the market was dominated by a handful of listed companies.

Uniqueness is different from rarity, happens infrequently, and commands the best possible price. A well known example of a unique company, which happens to be listed, is The Body Shop.

It must be realised, however, that uniqueness does not last for ever. There is always the possibility that a major company will use its financial, technical and marketing muscle to become an effective competitor within the medium term. So it is important to get the timing right when selling a company which is presently unique.

Defensive need to acquire

The defensive need to acquire may arise when a private company creates a new product, service or distribution network which is likely to threaten the existing business of a major company.

In these circumstances, the company under threat is likely

to take into account not only the additional profit resulting from the acquisition of the private company, but also the loss of existing profits if the competitor is allowed to continue. Once again, the advantage may prove to be only temporary, so the timing of the sale is important.

Sometimes, stock market listed companies feel themselves to be under pressure to make an acquisition either to diversify into more attractive market sectors or to reduce their own vulnerability to acquisition. If they believe this to be the case, whether it is a correct analysis or not, it is likely to encourage them to pay a somewhat more generous price as a result.

Upstream and downstream profit impact

Some banks and insurance companies have bought chains of estate agents at what seemed excessive prices in relation to the profits and net asset worth. There are two valuable benefits which have been gained. One is an exclusive distribution outlet for their own financial products, whereas previously the chain offered a variety of competing products. The other is that not only will profit be made from the sale of financial products by the estate agents, but there will be profit to the bank or insurance company as the supplier of these products.

It is important therefore to recognise upstream and downstream profit opportunities for an acquirer, which will benefit another subsidiary of the group, because this encourages the payment of a premium price.

The approach to valuation

By now it will be realised that there is much more to valuation than the use of formulae and yardsticks. None the less, rigorous financial analysis is the foundation, to which should be added insight and judgement. What is more, several methods of calculation should be used. It is definitely inadvisable to choose one favourite method of valuation, thereby rejecting other techniques.

Another vital point to emphasise is that the value placed on a given business is likely to be different from one prospective purchaser to the next. The particular valuation will depend on the ability to pay and the incremental benefits to be gained.

EXECUTIVE SUMMARY

▷ Individual vendors of private companies should assess whether the net capital sum to be received will allow early retirement and their present lifestyle to be maintained

▷ Fundamental valuation factors are the incremental profits and cash flow to be gained by a particular purchaser, and to a lesser extent, the worth of the assets acquired

▷ Adjusted profits, cash flows and balance sheets should be used for valuation calculations

▷ Several financial criteria should be used, including:
  • earnings multiples
  • discounted cash flow techniques
  • return on investment
  • impact on earnings per share
  • net asset backing, for a loss-making company

▷ Less quantifiable factors which affect prices paid include:
  • scarcity, rarity and uniqueness
  • a defensive need to acquire
  • upstream and downstream benefits

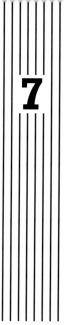

How to Find and Handle Prospective Purchasers

To avoid a waste of management time and the risk of damaging the business, once a valuation of the worth of the company has been made, the next steps should be:

▷ to confirm the decision to sell

▷ to set the minimum price acceptable

In the light of the valuation, it may make sense to delay the sale until either losses have been eliminated or current profits have been increased in order to achieve an acceptable price.

What may be less obvious is the importance of setting the minimum acceptable price. An agreement to sell a business needs to be based on a minimum price in order to be meaningful. If professional advisers think it is unlikely that the minimum price required will be obtainable, then the right decision may be to improve the business before selling it. To seek different professional advisers may be wrong. Some will glibly talk about an attractive price simply to win the assignment. The important thing is to find out the reasons and evidence for any views on valuation put forward by professional advisers.

FIND FIRST, CONTACT LATER

A pitfall to avoid is approaching one or two companies, perhaps chosen because of suitable personal contacts, reaching the point of final negotiation, and then involving professional advisers. They may believe that other purchasers would offer a significantly better price.

The clear message is:

> ▷ identify all prospective purchasers first, from both home and overseas

> ▷ decide the method of approach

> ▷ work to a timetable

Each of these steps will be considered in turn.

Identify prospective purchasers

It is essential to identify all likely purchasers at home and overseas, or in a few cases, decide that it is almost impossible to do so because of the small size and nature of the business.

Overseas purchasers are potentially attractive because there is definite evidence that companies do tend to pay higher prices when acquiring abroad. One possible reason is that it is more difficult to identify and handle acquisitions overseas, because of the logistical problems and the extra costs involved, so when an opportunity is found there is an extra determination to do a deal.

An actual example illustrates the improbability in a few cases of identifying prospective purchasers. The company in question sold Christmas gift hampers by mail order and made a profit before tax in excess of £100,000 a year. It was managed entirely by the owner, with the support of low-grade staff. An important feature of the product was the supply of attractive merchandise obtained direct from specialist suppliers in several countries. As a result of terminal illness, an urgent sale of the business was needed.

It was decided that companies already in the hamper

market may be unwilling to pay an attractive price. The view was taken that a private individual or company may be a more likely buyer, and that in this case an advertisement would be needed to reach the widest number of potential buyers.

The more usual ways of identifying prospective purchasers include:

> ▷ personal contacts

> ▷ business brokers

> ▷ registers

> ▷ specific research

Each of these will be considered separately.

PERSONAL CONTACTS

The directors of the company to be sold will be able to identify some prospective purchasers such as:

> ▷ previous approaches to buy the business which were rejected

> ▷ competitors

> ▷ major customers or suppliers

> ▷ companies which are complementary

An example of a complementary company is one which sells to the same customers or through the same distribution channels. A bathroom fitting importer, selling to do-it-yourself retail chains, may be attracted to a company selling home security products through the same outlets.

Perhaps the most difficult source of prospective purchasers to be identified from within the company are overseas buyers, simply because of a possible lack of involvement with them as customers, suppliers or competitors.

BUSINESS BROKERS

Business brokers may seem an ideal choice. After all, their prime job is the introduction of buyers and sellers to each other. It must be remembered, however, that their 'no deal—no fee' basis of rewards means they are motivated to complete deals and not necessarily to secure the best possible price or to be concerned about who is the purchaser. The deal is the thing for them.

Another factor to be considered is confidentiality. Some brokers are always ready to talk about possible deals, even gossip about them, to produce results. They may have reciprocal arrangements with other brokers to share fees when a sale results from an introduction by another broker.

So before appointing a business broker, obtain satisfactory answers to the following questions:

> will the identity of the company for sale be revealed only with specific approval?

> is the broker retained by any companies, or does the broker know of others, looking to acquire a similar business?

> what specific research will be done to identify other purchasers at home and overseas?

> how will the broker contact prospective purchasers, and screen them before a meeting with the vendors?

> who are three recent vendors willing to be telephoned as satisfied clients?

Some brokers pursue potential vendors aggressively. If they are not appointed immediately to handle the sale, they may seek to introduce prospective purchasers anyway to win the assignment or pull off a deal even if another company has been appointed.

REGISTERS

Banks, stockbrokers, chartered accountants, acquisition and disposal specialists and business brokers are amongst those who maintain registers of the requirements of acquirers and companies for sale. Usually, these are strictly confidential and remain unpublished.

A comprehensive list of buyers' requirements is useful. It may allow one or more prospective buyers to be identified immediately. An important feature is a register which includes the diversification plans of major companies. Otherwise, it may not be realised that a bookseller wishes to move into commercial stationery supply, or whatever. Importantly, companies eager to diversify into a specific sector may be ready to pay an attractive price.

The Livingstone Fisher Acquisition Register contains the confidential acquisition requirements of nearly a thousand companies wishing to acquire in the UK. Companies from many countries are included in the register.

None the less, it has to be said that a register should be regarded only as a valuable database to be used to complement specific research to locate prospective purchasers. Evidence shows that reliance on a register alone is unlikely to produce a sale.

Disposal registers should be viewed with suspicion by prospective vendors, because this is how purchasers look at them. There is a shortage of companies available to purchase which are worth buying, and a surfeit of willing purchasers in most business sectors. So it is not surprising that companies on disposal registers tend to be unattractive ones and often quite small.

SPECIFIC RESEARCH

There is no substitute for specific research to identify as many prospective purchasers as possible from home and overseas. In the recent sale of a UK-based pet-food manufacturer, interested purchasers included companies from mainland Europe, the USA and one in Australia.

It tends to be acquisition and disposal specialists who have the experience and resources to carry out this specific research. Before appointing one, as there will be a fee involved to demonstrate a commitment to sell, be satisfied that they have a proven competence, and will be able to handle each stage of the transaction through to legal completion.

Methods of approach

Having identified prospective purchasers, the possible methods of approach include:

▷ direct approach

▷ advertisement

▷ press release

▷ auction

In some cases, more than one avenue of approach will be used, but it is helpful to consider each separately.

DIRECT APPROACH

It is not unusual for specific research to identify between ten and twenty possible purchasers, and occasionally even a few more. The next step needs to be a grouping or classification, under categories such as:

▷ short list

▷ others

▷ reserve list

In order to maintain confidentiality, one or more competitors may be deliberately excluded from the short list and possibly kept on the reserve list.

The research work should identify the name of the individual to be contacted in each company. In a major multinational, it is more likely to be the person in charge of a group of related subsidiaries rather than the corporate chief executive officer. It is desirable, however, to contact an executive in charge rather than a corporate staff person.

The telephone is a more effective and flexible means of direct approach than a letter. If the specialist advisers are also involved in helping companies to achieve a flotation on a stock market and providing initial strategic advice, as are Livingstone Fisher and numerous others, it allows a possible sale to be portrayed accurately as one of the options being considered.

The purpose of the telephone conversation should simply be to establish a possible interest to purchase, without disclosing the identity of the vendors. The next step would be to have a confidentiality agreement signed by the prospective purchaser. The confidentiality agreement should:

> bind the professional advisers to the purchaser as well

> prevent any disclosure of information or indication of the possibility of a sale to a third party

> require the return of all documents provided, and any copies taken, unless the purchase is completed

None the less, a competitor can gain commercially valuable information merely by pursuing a possible acquisition.

Using the direct approach, it is desirable not to have more than three or four interested parties at any one time in order to be manageable 'in parallel' by the vendors, and to maintain as much confidentiality as possible.

PRESS ADVERTISEMENT

If it has been decided that specific research is unlikely to identify prospective purchasers, then press advertising should be considered, rather than relying on a register.

A decision needs to be made whether to advertise in a newspaper or a trade magazine. If the objective is to reach the widest possible spectrum of prospective purchasers, then a newspaper is probably more appropriate.

It is assumed that the identity of the company will not be disclosed. So the advert could be placed using a box number or in the name of an accountant, solicitor or specialist adviser.

To get the best possible response from an advert there are several features which should be included:

> a heading such as 'For Sale—Builders Merchant', unless the advertisement is to be inserted in a Business for Sale column, so that the nature of the advertisement is obvious

▷ a location, without being specific enough to reveal the identity of the company

▷ sales turnover, expressed approximately

▷ an indication of profitability, preferably profit before tax

▷ the name of the person handling the disposal and a telephone number to contact to make it easy for people to respond to the advert

Another avenue to consider when preparing an advert is to use the heading 'Builders Merchant—Acquisition, Merger or Sale'. This establishes that a sale of the business is only one of the options being considered.

PRESS RELEASE

A large company intending to sell a sizeable subsidiary or division may decide to issue a press release to the national and trade press announcing the disposal. This assumes that a definite decision to sell has been made, there will be several interested buyers and the people working in the business have been informed.

The press release—or press conference, if the disposal is sufficiently newsworthy—may include comments such as:

▷ a certain minimum price is expected

▷ an alternative being considered is a separate flotation of the business

▷ the disposal is being handled by a particular bank or specialist adviser so purchasers know who to contact

▷ an auction will be carried out and the sale is expected to be completed within a stated period

Work to a timetable

Whilst a business is being sold, a state of limbo exists. There is an understandable tendency to defer important capital expenditure, management recruitment and discretionary revenue items, such as expensive product literature. Also, the longer the sale process is allowed to take the greater is the risk of rumour and speculation amongst staff, customers and suppliers. So a realistic timetable should be set and adhered to.

Some banks and specialist advisers have demonstrated an ability to dispose of businesses by auction. An important feature of an auction is that a timetable is usually decided upon at the outset. In contrast, when a business is sold by direct approaches to prospective buyers there is often a tendency for events to drift. This is unacceptable, and should not be allowed to happen.

The auction and direct approach methods will be outlined in turn.

SALE BY AUCTION

The auction method is being used more widely, but it has been largely restricted to the disposal of subsidiaries and divisions by groups in the UK.

The approach is to notify all prospective purchasers simultaneously that a disposal is to be made. Whilst a press release to both the national and trade press should notify all prospective purchasers in the particular country, it has to be assumed that this will not achieve sufficient coverage overseas. So prospective purchasers overseas should be researched and approached direct at the same time. Alternatively, if it is considered that any press coverage would be undesirable, a direct approach should be made to companies at home as well as overseas.

Some auctions will produce more than twenty replies, and the aim should be quickly to reduce this number to two or three companies for serious negotiation.

The stages and timescales involved may be as follows:

Timescale	Stage
Week 1	Confidentiality agreements signed and detailed Memorandum of Sale despatched to principals and then advisers
Week 3	Outline written offers to be received
Week 4	Up to about five prospective purchasers short-listed
Weeks 5 and 6	Each shortlisted company allowed to spend a day with the management
Week 7	Outline written offers confirmed or amended
Week 8	Detailed negotiations completed

To accelerate legal completion, the vendors may prepare and present the purchase contract to be signed. Normally, of course, it is the lawyers to the purchaser who prepare the purchase contract. Dependent upon the size and method of financing the purchase, however, further time may be required to obtain stock exchange approval or shareholder agreement.

An important benefit of an auction is that a significantly higher price may be obtained.

SALE BY DIRECT APPROACH

The aim should be to approach sufficient prospective purchasers simultaneously so that between three and six companies have an initial meeting with the vendors, after a preliminary screening meeting with the specialist advisers.

An outline of the stages and timescale required is:

Timescale	Stage
Week 1	Prospective purchasers telephoned to establish up to six interested companies, and confidentiality agreements signed
Weeks 2 and 3	Outline description of business provided and preliminary screening by advisers
Weeks 4 and 5	Preliminary meetings with vendors

Weeks   Preferred purchaser given access to the company
6 and 7

Week 10   Detailed negotiations completed

Clearly, at least one other interested purchaser will be kept in reserve. It is unrealistic, however, to think that, say, three purchasers can be given detailed access to the business and that detailed negotiations can take place with each of them in parallel.

Memorandum for Sale

If the business is to be auctioned a comprehensive Memorandum for Sale is required. This has to contain sufficient information to enable prospective purchasers to make a meaningful outline written offer without visiting the premises or meeting the management.

Usually, the Memorandum for Sale will be written by the advisers to the company, based on information supplied to them by the management. The contents will need to include:

▷ executive summary

▷ description of the business

▷ history

▷ present and previous ownership

▷ market segments and countries served

▷ products and services

▷ manufacture or sources of supply

▷ major customers and distribution channels

▷ location and premises

▷ management and staff

▷ intellectual property

▷ reason for sale

▷ financial information

The financial information will need to include:

▷ profit and loss accounts for the previous three years

▷ current year budget and latest year end forecast

▷ future years' projections

▷ details of all intra-group charges

▷ cash flow projections

▷ latest balance sheet

▷ schedule of key assets

▷ statement of accounting policies

It must be remembered that the Memorandum for Sale should literally be a selling document. Future benefits and opportunities should be outlined.

OUTLINE DESCRIPTION OF THE BUSINESS

When a business is to be sold by a direct approach to prospective purchasers, the cost and time required to write a Memorandum for Sale should be avoided in most circumstances.

None the less, it is useful to have an Outline Description, probably no longer than four pages, to give to each prospective purchaser after a confidentiality agreement has been signed.

This ensures a uniformity in the information provided, and if specialist advisers are involved, gives a sufficient description to establish that the purchaser should meet the vendors.

The content of the Outline Description should be a much-abbreviated version of the Memorandum for Sale, but ensuring that no particularly commercially sensitive information is provided prematurely.

Vendors may believe that they should write the Outline Description. First-hand experience suggests otherwise. Vendors often describe their own business in an introspective way and fail to point out the attractive features and future opportunities which they take for granted.

SETTING THE ASKING PRICE

The setting and use of an asking price is a truly vexed question.

It is trite but true that a vendor who quotes a specific asking price is unlikely to receive a higher figure. So a balance has to be struck between avoiding the risk of setting too low a figure and, on the other hand, one so high that any chance of a sale is precluded.

Probably the safest way to express an asking price is to quote a range rather than a specific figure.

One thing is certain. The subject of purchase price should be raised, at least in broad terms, at the first meeting with a prospective purchaser. Unless there is a willingness to pay a satisfactory price, subject to seeing the business in more detail prior to detailed negotiations, there is no point in further meetings.

Vendors are often embarrassed at raising the question of purchase price at an initial meeting, or simply do not know how to handle it. The result is that they spend time giving much confidential information to a prospective purchaser, only to be shocked and upset if a totally unsatisfactory offer is made subsequently. If specialist advisers are involved, require them to raise the subject of price as part of the initial screening process.

The fact remains, however, that there is merit in persuading the prospective purchaser to indicate a likely price range and so avoid being the first to disclose a figure. If the price suggested is too low, then the asking price should be given in response. If the figure put forward is attractive, then the asking price should be increased!

HANDLING PURCHASER VISITS

Visits to company premises by prospective purchasers should be kept to an absolute minimum to minimise rumour and speculation.

The initial meeting between vendor and purchaser should *not* take place on the company premises.

The scope of the first meeting should be to:

> ▷ find out about the purchasing company, and their method of making acquisitions and managing them afterwards

> ▷ obtain details of any relevant acquisitions they have made during the previous three years

> ▷ find out what thoughts they have about developing the company under their ownership

> ▷ outline the benefits, opportunities and potential of the business

> ▷ avoid giving commercially sensitive information at this stage

If a decision to pursue matters is to be taken, then a visit to the premises will be required. None the less, it should be carefully controlled.

The visit to company premises should be restricted to seeing the facilities. The provision of detailed information can take place equally as well in a nearby hotel, provided adequate notice is given of what is desired. Furthermore, there may be departments such as research and development where it would be inappropriate to provide access until after a detailed verbal agreement for the sale has been reached.

During the brief visit to the premises any conversation and discussion should be restricted only to those people who are directly involved in the sale of the business.

There may be detailed information requested which is commercially sensitive and this should only be given when oral negotiations have been completed. When dealing with a competitor, this issue becomes more important still.

Information which may be commercially sensitive includes:

> ▷ specific details about the mix of business, volumes, prices and discounts with major customers

> ▷ process know-how, especially where patent protection does not exist

> ▷ details of new product development or research projects

> ▷ sources of supply from overseas, where no exclusive supply agreement exists

External accountants should *not* be allowed to carry out an on-site investigation until detailed oral negotiations have been completed and a draft purchase contract has been received. Yet vendors sometimes allow it to happen. Specialist advisers would not. It is extremely difficult, if not impossible, to avoid rumour, speculation and probably the knowledge that the business is to be sold during an accountancy investigation.

EXECUTIVE SUMMARY

> ▷ Identify all likely purchasers from home and overseas using specific research, before contacting any of them

> ▷ Evidence shows that overseas purchasers are likely to pay higher prices

> ▷ If a business broker is to be used, insist on telephoning two or three recent clients

> ▷ Be wary of placing a business for sale on a Disposal Register, because prospective purchasers tend to be even more wary of them

> ▷ The telephone is an effective way of making a direct approach to a prospective purchaser

▷ An auction is an effective method of selling a subsidiary or division of a group, based on a comprehensive Memorandum for Sale

▷ The sale of a private company should be carried out within a broad timetable, and it is useful to prepare an Outline Description of the business

▷ The question of purchase price should be raised, in broad terms, at the first meeting

▷ Visits to the company premises should be kept to a minimum

How to Negotiate a Deal

8

Negotiation is an art not a science. Furthermore, negotiating the sale of a business is deceptively complex. It requires an awareness of the relevant taxation and legal regulations in the country concerned. Otherwise, unknowingly, a seemingly attractive deal may be negotiated, with onerous tax consequences or unacceptable legal implications.

Earn-out deals add another level of complexity. Some people mistakenly think that the drafting of the earn-out formulae can be safely left to experienced lawyers. It can, but only if the details have been resolved between the purchasers and vendors first.

Emotional involvement is a problem for the vendors of a private company. The degree of personal turmoil is comparable to an acrimonious divorce. An unacceptably low offer or a critical comment about the company may well be treated as a personal insult. People selling a business for a multinational group may be equally lacking in previous experience of negotiating acquisitions and disposals. They may be senior executives, but still come off second best against expert professional advisers.

Countless vendors of private companies have said words

to the effect that 'I never want to go through an experience like that again'. In one case, when the purchaser withdrew for seemingly inadequate reasons less than a week before legal completion, the owner said 'it will be several years before I can face selling the company again'.

If negotiations are about to take place, and professional advisers have not been appointed, the unequivocal advice is to consider appointing them immediately.

There are three key features for negotiating the sale of a business successfully:

▷ establishing the deal format

▷ negotiating the price and other features

▷ agreeing the forms of purchase consideration

Each of these will be considered separately.

THE DEAL FORMAT

Two extremes are to be avoided in negotiating the sale of a business. Firstly, negotiations which are spread out over several months with one purchaser. This is quite unnecessary and unacceptable. Secondly, being persuaded into ('hustled into' is a more accurate phrase) commencing and completing negotiations in a single meeting.

A two-stage approach is strongly recommended:

▷ an initial meeting to agree a deal format and, subject to satisfactory agreement, to set a date for

▷ a detailed negotiation meeting to agree the price and key features so that lawyers can be instructed to draft the contract

Key elements of the format for a deal include:

▷ what is to be sold

▷ outright sale or earn-out deal

▷ the price range

> ▷ purchase of assets

> ▷ key conditions

> ▷ management continuity

> ▷ profit warranties

Each of these will be considered in turn.

What is to be sold

One possibility the purchasers may suggest is that assets and intellectual property are sold rather than the share capital of the company. This has the attraction for the purchaser that any skeletons in the cupboard are safely left behind. From the vendor's viewpoint, a sale of assets may be less attractive because of taxation problems.

If the assets of a private company are sold rather than the equity, only a shell will remain containing the proceeds of the sale. The purchasers will insist, however, that the name of the company is transferred to them and that the vendors cease trading immediately. So in some countries there will be extra tax payable to extract the proceeds of the sale from the company for the benefit of the individual shareholders.

Whenever a group intends to dispose of the assets and intellectual property of a business, expert advice should be taken before the decision is made to ensure that tax liabilities are minimised.

If some property is owned by individual shareholders, and used by the business, they may prefer to grant only a short lease in order to retain the development potential which exists from the possibility of obtaining permission for alternative use or because of future road construction which will increase the value of the premises.

A particular subsidiary or part of the business may not be of interest or attractive to the purchaser. The vendors should not overlook the opportunity to exclude it from the sale, with little impact on the purchase price to be obtained, and then either to retain it for themselves or to sell it at an attractive price separately. In an actual case, a business consisted of a chain of retail travel agents and a small but specialised inclusive tour operator. The purchaser only wanted the travel agency and was so keen to avoid the problems of managing a tour operator that it was agreed to exclude it at the deal format stage for a nominal sum. Two years later the tour operator was sold for a handsome price.

It may be necessary for a group to retain intellectual property rights, such as patents or brand names, for use elsewhere in the group and to grant a licence to the purchaser for particular use in certain countries.

Outright sale or earn-out deal

If the vendors expect an outright purchase, then this should be confirmed at the meeting to discuss the deal format. It would be quite unacceptable to discover at the detailed negotiation stage that the only deal being offered is an earn-out one. Equally, it should be established that there will be no question of a retention of part of the purchase price for a given period after legal completion as a form of security for the warranties and indemnities to be given.

If an earn-out deal has been agreed in principle, then some of the features needing preliminary discussion are:

> the percentage of equity to be purchased initially—if less than 100 per cent is to be purchased initially, it is essential to ensure that the vendors will have the right to oblige the purchaser to buy the remainder within a given period, in addition to the purchaser having similar rights. Expert tax advice is necessary to ensure that no additional capital gains tax liability will be crystallised immediately

> the period of the earn-out—it can be argued that the shorter the earn-out period the better it is for vendors, and generally this will be true. Earn-out periods of longer than two years after the end of the current financial year should be strongly resisted. Longer than two more years may turn out to seem like a life sentence, and the

likelihood of unforeseeable external factors which depress profits increases significantly beyond this period

▷   the proportion of earn-out payments—in extreme cases earn-out deals have been completed where more than 90 per cent of the total purchase price has been dependent upon future performance. In contrast, some deals have earn-out payments of less than 10 per cent. With this range of possibilities, it is essential to discuss the proportion of earn-out payments which will apply

Some purchasers propose an initial payment on an earn-out deal of less than the present net asset worth of the company. If the company is profitable, this should be categorically rejected. The aim should be to get an initial payment which fully reflects the worth of the business today. The earn-out payments should reflect an additional bonus for further profit achievement.

Price range

At the deal format stage, the aim is not to negotiate a purchase price, but to establish a satisfactory price range. This may be quite wide, such as between £3 million and £5 million. Unless the lower figure is an acceptable one at which to complete a deal, there is no point in arranging a detailed negotiation meeting.

Purchase of assets

Sometimes in the sale of a private company, the vendors will either wish, or be asked by the purchaser, to buy certain assets which are not really needed for the running of the business. Boats, aeroplanes and expensive motor cars may come into this category and should present no problem.

Occasionally, something more unusual is involved. In one situation, a private company purchased a piece of land at the back of the site because it gave important access to land owned by the shareholders, and more importantly, they could not afford to buy it as individuals at the time. On this occasion, it was important to establish that the land would be excluded from the sale of the company, in order to retain the access.

Key conditions

It would be entirely wrong to get into detailed discussion about warranties and indemnities at the deal format stage. None the less, it is desirable to establish whether the purchaser is seeking any conditions which may be regarded as onerous, because it could be that these are totally unacceptable.

An example of this was the demand made by a purchaser that during a three-year earn-out period, earlier payments could be clawed back if subsequent profit thresholds were not achieved. To compound matters, the repayment was to include not only the original amount earned, but an interest penalty as well. Some plain speaking was needed to establish that such a condition was so unacceptable that it would become a 'deal breaker' if pursued.

Management continuity

When payment is in full on legal completion, if the vendors wish to retire then the aim should be to agree the shortest reasonable period of continuity.

If one or more of the vendors is seeking a career with the larger group, then this should be discussed and a period for an initial service contract agreed.

Profit warranties

This may be the final point raised by the purchasers, and it carries a sting in the tail. The vendors may be asked to warrant pre-tax profits for the current financial year. If such a warranty is to be considered by the vendors, the first thing to be established is the penalty for failure to meet the warranted profit figure. In some cases, the penalty suggested has been as high as seven times the amount of the shortfall.

If profits are to be warranted, and the penalty for a shortfall is in any way onerous, then the figure warranted should be one that is easily achievable. Otherwise, instead of accepting a penalty for a shortfall, it is better for the vendors to seek an earn-out payment on any excess profit over the figure suggested for a warranty.

If the deal format meeting produces a satisfactory basis for detailed negotiation, then it makes sense to agree a date for the detailed negotiations. This should allow sufficient time for the vendors to be adequately prepared and advised. Equally, it is important to establish that the purchaser will have the requisite authority by that date. For example, the purchaser may be required to obtain formal approval to negotiate at the next group board meeting.

In a case involving a multinational electronics company, the vendors were badly treated in this respect. Detailed negotiations took place, a draft contract was sent to the vendors and the accountancy investigation commenced. Three weeks after the negotiations, the purchaser announced that the main board had instructed that the offer be reduced by 25 per cent. Not surprisingly, the sale was never completed, but it was an unfortunate experience which is to be avoided.

NEGOTIATING THE DEAL

Detailed negotiations may require typically between three and twelve hours, sometimes longer. If much less than three hours is taken, there is a likelihood that some important issues have not been addressed.

It is desirable that the negotiations take place on neutral ground, perhaps in the offices of a professional adviser or in a hotel. A soundproof room, with a direct dial telephone, should be available for either side to adjourn.

A pre-negotiation meeting is strongly recommended. It ensures that everyone has assembled and is briefed on their role. A leader of the negotiation team should have been agreed upon.

Certain ground rules will have been established:

▷ no one will interrupt when a member of the other side is speaking, because a valuable point may be missed

▷ when a question is asked of the other side, the person will be allowed to answer it in full

▷ the negotiation team leader will interrupt one of his own team members if necessary

▷ the temptation to become irritated or to score points will be resisted

▷ the emphasis will be on listening

Before the negotiating meeting, a draft agenda should be prepared. If the purchasers have prepared one as well, then the agenda for the meeting needs to be agreed at the outset. The agenda should be designed to ensure that all the issues needed to produce a meaningful agreement will be discussed and agreed.

A typical agenda could be:

▷ update of events since last meeting

▷ assets and business to be purchased

▷ leases to be agreed

▷ assets to be purchased by vendors

▷ service contracts

▷ consultancy agreements

▷ retirement packages

▷ earn-out deal structure

▷ purchase price and consideration

▷ timetable to legal completion

Some of these need to be considered separately.

Update of events

The opportunity must not be lost to confirm continued progress by the business since the last meeting. This could include:

> ▷ the latest set of monthly management accounts
> ▷ orders received
> ▷ sales figures for the month which has just ended
> ▷ important press coverage
> ▷ the successful launch of a new product or service
> ▷ a major new customer

Leases to be agreed

If freehold property is to be excluded from the sale, then the main provisions of a lease should be agreed. It is sufficient to agree the type of lease, the duration, the annual value and rent review dates. The remaining details should be left to the lawyers to draft.

Assets to be purchased by the vendors

The opportunity should be taken to obtain any assets to be purchased at an attractive price. As has been mentioned, these may include boats, aeroplanes, cars and surplus land or property.

Service contracts

The reality is that a group purchaser will be keen to ensure that salaries, motor cars and fringe benefits are in line with group policy. When someone is being asked to continue in full-time employment for a year or more after an outright sale, to provide management continuity, it is worth seeking to negotiate a profit-linked bonus for this period.

Consultancy agreement

Certain directors may wish to retire from full-time employment on legal completion, but be available on an agreed basis for a given period. If so, the duration, duties, time to be spent, payment and expenses should be agreed so that a consultancy agreement can be prepared.

Retirement packages

The purchaser may require certain directors to leave immediately, even though they would prefer to continue. If so, it is worth pursuing a retirement package as compensation for loss of office. This requires a detailed knowledge of the taxation rules for the particular country.

Earn-out deals

Earn-out deals are a potential minefield for vendors. It is arguably more important to the purchaser, however, to produce an earn-out deal which works amicably in practice, because their purpose is presumably to ensure the continued motivation of the vendors. None the less many purchasers, who should know better, enter into earn-out deals lacking in clarity which are likely to cause disagreement later.

The issues which need to be addressed include:

▷ initial payment

▷ business development

▷ finance costs

▷ dividends

▷ cost rationalisation

▷ management charges

▷ central service charges

▷ intra-group trading

> ▷ accounting policies

> ▷ profit targets

> ▷ payment formula and limits

Each of these needs to be considered separately.

INITIAL PAYMENT

The first thing to be agreed in any earn-out deal is the initial percentage of equity to be purchased, which probably will be 100 per cent, and the amount to be paid. Unless this is acceptable, and reflects fully the value of the business today, there is no point in further discussion.

BUSINESS DEVELOPMENT

Vendors and purchasers alike need to outline their ideas for the development of the business during the earn-out period. The vendors will want to be satisfied that their plans for profit-able expansion, and the finance required, are supported by the purchasers. In contrast, they will wish to learn about any diversification or overseas development plans of the purchasers, if these could adversely affect profits during the earn-out period. If so, then it may be necessary to negotiate that these activities become part of a separate division which is to be excluded from the earn-out calculations.

FINANCE COSTS

Many large groups electronically sweep clean the bank account of each subsidiary every evening, by transferring the balance to a group account. This means that the rate of interest to be credited on surplus funds generated and to be charged on borrowings must be agreed. Usually, this is expressed in terms of the number of percentage points difference from the bank rate at any time.

DIVIDENDS

Some groups levy a dividend charge on their subsidiaries, especially overseas ones. This needs to be defined, because it will deplete cash resources and increase financing costs.

COST RATIONALISATION

It may be agreed that some cost rationalisation should take place after the sale, for example the closure of a branch or staff redundancy. If so, either an estimate of the cost needs to be agreed so that it can be included in the profit targets, along with the subsequent savings, or the costs should be borne by the purchasers.

MANAGEMENT CHARGES

The purchaser may require that administrative matters such as legal services, payroll preparations and pension arrangements are handled centrally, and a charge levied for the service. More importantly, some groups levy a charge to subsidiaries reflecting the cost of certain central functions such as research and development or publicity. These charges must be known before profit targets can be discussed meaningfully.

CENTRAL SERVICE CHARGES

The group may provide some services centrally which are charged on a usage basis. Examples include departments such as transport and data processing. Clearly, the effect these charges will have on future profits must be assessed.

INTRA-GROUP TRADING

Some groups operate an entirely 'arms-length' basis of trading between subsidiaries, which means there is no obligation at all to trade with each other. When any trade is done, no preferential pricing is expected.

Other groups operate differently. They require that subsidiaries must trade with each other and have a transfer pricing policy. The company being sold may already do business with the group, and so the prices will be affected. Also, it may be required to buy from other group companies, at higher prices than could be obtained elsewhere. Once again, the profit impact of these arrangements must be assessed.

ACCOUNTING POLICIES

As soon as legal completion takes place, it must be assumed that group accounting policies will come into effect and the group auditors will be appointed. It should not be assumed, however, that earn-out payments must automatically be based on accounts prepared by group auditors using group accounting policies.

There is considerable merit in negotiating that, for the purposes of calculating earn-out payments, the existing auditors will prepare the accounts using existing accounting policies. In this way, it is not necessary to assess the profit impact of different accounting policies, and any disagreement about their interpretation will be avoided.

PROFIT TARGETS

Before profit targets or thresholds are discussed, the amount expected to be earned in total should be agreed. Otherwise, there is a risk of agreeing to profit thresholds which are too high.

Purchasers are likely to want to set rising profit thresholds each year. Vendors should seek to negotiate a constant profit target based on the figure forecast for the current financial year. The crucial thing is that these figures take into account the profit effect of the factors outlined above.

PAYMENT FORMULA AND LIMITS

The understandable fear of any purchaser is that the vendors in an earn-out deal could adopt a wholly short-term approach in order to maximise the amount they receive. So a purchaser is likely to press for an upper limit on the earn-out payments. Provided this is sufficiently generous, the principle should be accepted.

The earn-out payment formula is likely to be based on a given multiple of the pre-tax profit in excess of a given figure. As well as seeking to increase the multiple, vendors should seek an additional lump sum for achieving the threshold figure each year, especially if the thresholds increase annually.

Purchase price and consideration

If the purchase is to be an earn-out deal, the price will have been agreed.

If it is an outright purchase, then this is the stage for the price to be agreed in the light of the agreement already reached on the other aspects of the sale outlined above.

It is at this stage that negotiation skills are of the essence. An attractive offer may well be greeted with a sense of dismay. An adjournment will probably be requested. No attempt must be made to rush into an agreement.

Once the purchase price has been agreed the form of consideration needs to be discussed. It is important that vendors realise that the range of possible options includes:

▷ retirement packages

▷ one-off pension contributions

▷ advantageous purchase of assets

▷ consultancy agreements

▷ purchase consideration

Several of these items have already been covered. Whilst one-off lump-sum pension contributions may be tax effective, pension planning should have already occurred prior to the sale. What is more, vendors usually add back directors pensions when doing their adjusted profit calculations.

The forms of purchase consideration available require separate examination.

PURCHASE CONSIDERATION

The consideration could be paid in various forms including:

▷ cash

▷ unquoted shares

▷ quoted shares

▷ loanstock

▷ convertible loanstock

A decision to accept shares in an unquoted company requires careful consideration. By the time of legal completion, the purchaser will have subjected the business being bought to thorough scrutiny as a result of the accountancy investigation. In contrast, the vendors will have relatively little authoritative knowledge about the current and future prospects of the purchasing company. Their firm intentions may be to seek a stock market quotation within one or two years, but unforeseeable events could delay this by several years. It has to be said that taking the purchase consideration wholly in the shares of an unquoted company remains something of a gamble.

Purchase consideration taken wholly in shares of a quoted company is less of a gamble, but may still represent a significant risk. This applies particularly in the case of a smaller quoted company where the opportunity to sell a sizeable number of shares simply may not exist, because of the limited volume of dealing in the shares. Also, it means that the proceeds of the sale are invested in only one share, and it must make sense to spread the investment risk. When a significant amount of shares is to be received in a quoted company, the vendors are often asked to agree not to sell any shares for one or two years. In the space of less than a year, the shares of a quoted company may halve or double in value. This must not be overlooked.

Vendors are understandably keen to avoid or defer capital gains tax liability on the sale of their company. Shares in the purchasing company will defer any liability, but either loanstock or convertible loanstock will do so as well.

Loanstock carries a given rate of interest, usually paid half-yearly, and should be repayable in full at the end of a given period. Repayment may typically be within three to five years. It is vital to be satisfied that the company will be in a financial position to redeem the loanstock on the agreed date, and when dealing with a smaller quoted company consideration should be given to seeking a guarantee of repayment by a major bank.

Convertible loanstock may offer a lower rate of interest than loanstock, but give the opportunity to convert the loanstock during a given period at a pre-determined, and hopefully attractive, price. For example, if the shares of the purchaser are quoted at 100p at the time of legal completion, conversion may be available at, say, 150p during the fourth year. Provided that the shares are priced higher than this in the market at the time, then this is a valuable option to have. It is important however, that there should be the opportunity to redeem the convertible loan stock on a given date just in case the conversion terms do not turn out to be attractive.

Timetable to legal completion

Assuming that satisfactory agreement has been reached, the final stage of the meeting is to agree an outline timetable culminating in the date of legal completion.

Vendors must realise that there is absolutely no cause whatsoever for celebration until legal completion takes place.

Some vendors selling to a management buy-out team have found the management deliberately delaying legal completion in an attempt to re-negotiate a better deal. Some vendors of private companies have found a quoted company delaying legal completion in order to issue a stock exchange circular covering another acquisition as well, particularly if some share placing with institutional investors is required to fund both purchases.

The detail of the timetable will be covered in the next chapter.

Overseas residency

Individual vendors who are to retire from the business immediately may wish to consider establishing overseas residency to avoid capital gains tax.

The fundamental point to be addressed is whether the shareholder and his or her family will be happy living abroad. A country may appear to offer an attractive lifestyle to a holidaymaker. The reality as a resident may be different. Language difficulties, medical needs, cultural differences and different lifestyles are some of the factors which must be considered carefully.

The other problem is taxation itself. In some countries, the taxation rules require that overseas residency needs to be established before legal completion. Furthermore, a period of up to three years abroad may be advised to ensure tax problems are avoided later. One thing is certain: expert tax advice is needed long before legal completion.

EXECUTIVE SUMMARY

> ▷ The negotiations to sell a business require a knowledge of the relevant taxation and legal rules in the country concerned

> ▷ A two-stage approach is recommended:
> - establish the deal format in outline
> - negotiate the detailed agreement

> ▷ Key elements of the deal format include:
> - what is to be sold
> - essential features of an earn-out deal
> - price range
> - key conditions

> ▷ An agenda helps to ensure that all the issues are addressed at the detailed negotiation meeting

> ▷ Some of the detailed features of an earn-out deal to be clarified are:
> - future development of the business
> - cost of finance
> - management charges
> - central service costs
> - intra-group pricing policy
> - accounting policies
> - profit targets and payment formula

> ▷ Possible forms of tax-effective purchase consideration may include:
> - retirement packages
> - lump-sum pension contributions

- a pre-completion dividend
- advantageous purchase of assets
- shares, loanstock and convertible loanstock

9

How to Handle Legal Completion

There is many a slip not only between cup and lip but also between verbal agreement and legal completion. This is a short chapter, and a vital one.

The first and important step towards legal completion should take place at the end of the verbal negotiation meeting, when the timetable to completion is agreed.

TIMETABLE TO COMPLETION

The timetable will usually include dates for:

▷ the signing of a heads of agreement or letter of intent, subject to contract

▷ the receipt of the draft purchase contract

▷ the receipt of supplementary agreements such as leases and service contracts

▷ the commencement and completion of the accountancy investigation work on-site

▷ the receipt by the purchaser of the accountant's report

> ▷ a date reserved for a meeting with the principals and lawyers present to resolve contractual matters

> ▷ the receipt of the disclosure statement

> ▷ the legal completion and signing of documents

This may seem somewhat hopeful. It should not be. Realistic dates should be agreed, which people are committed to achieve. Accountants and lawyers must realise that they are working to strict deadlines.

Each of the items will be considered separately.

Heads of agreement

Heads of agreement, sometimes referred to as a letter of intent, are not essential. At the least, however, it is important to have a written record of all the matters which have been agreed. This ensures a common understanding of what has been agreed, and serves to brief the lawyers.

Some purchasers, and some vendors too, like to make a little ceremony of the signing of heads of agreement. It should be recognised that:

> ▷ heads of agreement are usually non-binding, that is they are subject to contract and to a satisfactory accountancy investigation

> ▷ whilst it is useful to let a lawyer check the wording before signature, heads of agreement do not need to be written up in the precise legal style of the purchase contract

> ▷ the purchaser may include a paragraph to preclude the vendor's having discussions with another prospective purchaser or announcing the proposed sale before the date of legal completion

Draft purchase contract

The draft purchase contract will probably be at least fifty pages long, and may exceed one hundred pages if a complex earn-out deal is involved.

Vendors should take the trouble to read the purchase contract, although it is likely to seem boring and unnecessarily pedantic. At the meeting with their lawyer, they should obtain clarification of paragraphs which are unclear and hear which points the lawyer is unhappy about.

It must be realised that warranties and indemnities concerning taxation matters are commonplace, and offer relatively little room for negotiation. In essence, the purchaser will require recompense if unexpected tax liabilities arise for up to six years after legal completion.

Important issues to be negotiated are the maximum extent of the value of indemnity to be given and the *de minimis* limit, below which no claim can be pursued. Given the costs of litigation, it is in the interests of both parties to have a reasonably high *de minimis* limit.

Purchasers will not withdraw warranties or indemnities from the contract because the vendors say that everything is in order and therefore it would be superfluous to include them in the contract. Equally unacceptable will be the suggestion that a warranty or indemnity should be omitted because the purchasers are aware that it cannot be given because of known circumstances. They will require the vendors to reveal the matter in the disclosure statement.

After the initial meeting between the vendors and their lawyers to discuss the draft contract, it is desirable that the two sets of lawyers amend and agree as much of the contract as possible between themselves.

Supplementary agreements

Service contracts for the continued employment of certain directors will be written in the standard format used by the purchasing company. Negotiation is likely to be restricted mainly to the amount of salary, length of contract, and period of notice.

Lease agreements should be relatively uncontentious in wording, compared with the importance of the purchase contract.

Loanstock or convertible loanstock agreements need to be considered carefully and re-negotiated as appropriate to provide sufficient safeguards for the vendors.

Accountancy investigation

It is recommended that the accountancy investigation is not scheduled, or allowed, to commence until there has been sufficient time to consider the draft contract. It is unlikely, but does happen occasionally, that the contract contains items which had not been discussed and are completely unacceptable. One such example was a retention of 20 per cent of the purchase consideration for two years.

The accountancy investigation requires considerable time spent on company premises. The minimum scale is likely to be two people on site for a week, and could be much larger and longer for a sizeable and complex sale.

The investigating accountants will need access to the senior finance person within the business. Furthermore, they are likely to need to come into contact with other people. For example, if a review of the current year's profit forecast is to be performed, they may ask to interview senior sales and production management.

It is during the accountancy investigation that rumour and speculation that the business is being sold are likely to occur. The influx of people asking lots of questions prompts speculation, so it is important that the scope, duration and scale of the accountancy investigation should be agreed when the timetable to legal completion is being set.

Accountants' report

Even though it is highly unusual for the vendors to be allowed to see the investigating accountants' report, it is worth knowing when it is expected. This should help to eliminate a possible excuse for delaying legal completion. Also, it enables contact to be made to check that the accountants' report is satisfactory, as was to be expected.

The purchasers may respond differently. In an extreme case, they may withdraw from the deal and only give a broad outline of their reasons. More often, the purchasers may seek to negotiate a lower price or to switch to an earn-out deal as a result of the investigation. This is the time for the vendors to demonstrate resolve.

If the vendors were honest and open when discussing the business with the purchasers prior to negotiation, then it should be possible to state that the items were known about previously. If important features were not outlined accurately or omitted, then the vendors should expect re-negotiation, and if sufficiently serious, then the withdrawal of the purchaser.

A point worth making to purchasers is that accountants' reports tend to be critical by the nature of the exercise. Also, some accountancy firms have faced expensive litigation as a result of shortcomings not uncovered during their investigation, which makes them cautious when writing their report on the business.

Contract agreement

It is unlikely that the two sets of lawyers will be able to reach a final agreement of the whole draft contract without the intervention of the principals. There are likely to be at least a few material points to be resolved.

It is for this reason that it is advisable to reserve a date for a meeting to resolve any outstanding contractual matters. If this is not included as part of the timetable, the problem of people not being available for a meeting could delay legal completion.

Before the meeting takes place, it is important that the

vendors have been briefed on the outstanding points and the differences of opinion which exist on each one. The principals and their advisers should be at the meeting, and it is important that sufficient time is available to neotiate an agreement on all outstanding points. Then, after the meeting, the lawyers can be left to amend and agree the wording of the contract.

Disclosure statement

The onus is on the vendors to disclose circumstances which breach the warranties given in the contract. This is done in the form of a disclosure statement, prepared by the vendors' lawyers based on information provided by them. Care must be taken to ensure that all relevant disclosures are made.

Sometimes the lawyers do not present the disclosure statement until the day of legal completion. This can cause unwanted problems on what should be an enjoyable day. The purchasers may find some parts of the disclosure statement too broad to be acceptable. This could lead to substantial rewriting of the disclosure statement, not to mention some harsh words being spoken, before legal completion takes place.

On the other hand, there is a case for presenting the disclosure statement at the final meeting to resolve any outstanding points when the principals are present. A knowledge of exactly what is to be disclosed, and the wording to be used, can make agreement of the oustanding points more easily reached. It has to be said, however, that opinions differ amongst experienced professionals on how best to handle disclosure statements.

Legal completion

Legal completion should be an enjoyable day for both sides. When a private company is sold, it marks the end of an era for the vendors. They are parting with an important slice of their lives.

Too often the day of legal completion is boring and tense. Boring because the lawyers may arrive at the same time as the principals, and then spend two or three hours sorting out the documentation and clearing up technical details. All of which should have been done before. It is worth asking the lawyers to arrive two or three hours earlier, if they feel it is necessary, in order to have everything ready.

Worse still, the disclosure statement may need some rewriting and there may be one or two contentious legal points still outstanding. This really does detract from the occasion of legal completion. At the final meeting to agree the outstanding points of difference remaining in the contract, both sets of lawyers should be asked to ensure a speedy and smooth legal completion meeting.

Lastly, a subjective comment. Midday is an excellent time to sign the documents for legal completion. Why? Because there is time for a celebratory glass of champagne or two before an enjoyable lunch with the purchasers!

EXECUTIVE SUMMARY

▷ A timetable to legal completion should be agreed at the end of the detailed negotiation meeting

▷ Heads of agreement are normally subject to contract, which means they are non-binding. While they are not essential, they are desirable

▷ Warranties and indemnities concerning all taxation matters are included in purchase contracts

▷ The accountancy investigation should not be allowed to commence until the draft contract has been received

▷ A meeting may be required, with the principals present, to resolve outstanding differences in the contract which the lawyers cannot agree upon

▷ Care must be taken to give comprehensive and accurate information in the disclosure statement

▷ Last-minute preparation needs to be done by the lawyers to ensure a brief and enjoyable legal completion meeting

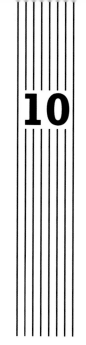

How to Eliminate Losses Before Selling

It is surprising how often both listed groups and private companies choose to sell when the subsidiary or business is making a loss.

This is probably the worst possible time to sell. The best possible return on investment has to be to turn the business back into profits during the next twelve months, and then to consider a sale. Not only may the business have proved unsaleable before, but a substantially higher price should be obtained.

In many ways it is easier for a group to turn round a subsidiary than to achieve the same result in a private company. A group should be able to transfer a proven executive to carry out the turn-around. For a private company, it requires the directors to take some painful decisions quickly. There is no time to lose. What is needed, however, is a proven framework for turning round a loss maker.

Urgent and decisive action is essential. In a loss-making business, as with a road-accident victim, the first step is to stop the bleeding.

This is obvious and common sense. Unfortunately, too often the response is indecision and procrastination. In one group with a turnover of over £1 billion, analysis showed that the worst performing subsidiaries had produced a sizeable aggregate loss in each of the previous two years. These subsidiaries accounted for over a third of total group turnover, and the current year forecast showed little improvement for them; yet the group board displayed no sense of urgency to tackle the problem. Good results in the remainder of the group meant that overall performance was satisfactory, but it could have been much better.

Unless the chief executive of a loss-making company has a convincing plan to restore success as quickly as is possible in the particular circumstances which exist, he should be removed promptly. The problem is that people with a record of managing successful companies to achieve greater success often have no experience of turning round loss-making companies. The management style required is very different. In a successful company a newly appointed chief executive will take time before making significant changes, but in a turn-around situation the new person must make his impact felt from the first day.

The new chief executive needs to be full-time, and a substantial amount of overtime will be required initially. He will need the support of an experienced financial manager. If one does not exist within the business, then someone should be provided immediately, on a temporary secondment from elsewhere within the group if necessary.

A programme is necessary to ensure that progress is achieved quickly. An outline programme could be:

Day 1   Take financial control and make an impact.

Week 1   Deal urgently with any cash flow crisis which threatens survival.
Assess the financial performance in broad terms.
Initiate financial analysis as a basis for making short-term decisions.
Start to decide the level of initial cost reduction necessary.

Month 1   Investigate each area of the business.
Decide the level of cost reduction required in each function.
Ask people to make specific recommendations to achieve the cost reduction required.
Make preparations for the headcount reductions needed.
Carry out the headcount reductions needed.

Month 2   Initiate short-term profit improvement projects.
Set a budget for the remainder of the financial year.

Month 3   Begin to create the vision for future success.
Define major business development projects to create an adequate return on funds invested.

The actual timing will depend upon the size and complexity of the business.

THE FIRST DAY

Urgency must be displayed at the outset. Financial control must be secured immediately. Initially, strict scrutiny will apply to:

▷ placing purchase orders

▷ signing cheques

▷ recruitment, including replacing people who leave

▷ foreign travel

An impact needs to be made. Some items of avoidable and non-essential expense should be terminated immediately. If it is damaging the business, someone will complain. Examples where immediate cost reduction should be made include:

▷ personal expenses—lavish meals, expensive hotels and first class travel should be replaced by a more modest approach. There should be no exception allowed. The chief executive must set a personal example

> ▷ temporary staff—all temporary staff should be terminated immediately unless they are revenue-earning or essential to serve the customer

> ▷ company cars—cars should be replaced only when the cost of repair becomes unacceptable

> ▷ discretionary expenses—plans for items such as re-equipping staff canteens, painting offices and other non-essential expenditure should be delayed

THE FIRST WEEK

If there is a cash flow crisis threatening the survival of the business immediate action must be taken. This may include:

> ▷ using senior managers and partners to collect overdue debts by telephone call or personal visit wherever appropriate, concentrating on large amounts which can be received quickly

> ▷ negotiations with bankers and others to secure additional finance or an increased overdraft facility

> ▷ negotiations with tax authorities to avoid legal action for overdue payments and to agree a phased payment schedule, provided that penal interest rates are not charged

> ▷ paying only those invoices necessary to avoid legal action and to ensure continuity of essential supplies and services

> ▷ seeking extended credit terms from major suppliers wherever appropriate

Much of this action may only be needed temporarily.

The rest of the first week should be spent searching out the reasons for making a loss.

Sometimes the required financial analysis is not available to highlight the extent of the problem. In one turn-around situation, in the silicon chip industry, only out-of-date costs were available, the current actual product costs were not known. Falling prices caused by rapid technological change and surplus capacity elsewhere in the industry meant that some products were being sold for less than the standard product cost, on the assumption that at least a reasonable marginal profit was being made. An urgent and necessarily approximate marginal cost analysis showed that the market price for the best selling product had fallen below marginal cost. Every unit of this product which was sold increased the loss, and the more that were sold the bigger became the loss. Drastic and urgent action had to be taken.

Other problems may include a shortage of orders, inaccurate contract cost estimating, inefficient production, costly subcontract work and excessive overhead levels. A swift decision on the immediate level of cost reduction needs to be made.

THE FIRST MONTH

The remainder of the first month should be spent assessing each aspect of the business at first hand. By the end of the month, preparation for any headcount reductions required should have been made. If the law requires a minimum period of notice to be given before redundancies can be made, then the need for urgency is even greater.

Sales

The sales department, rather than marketing, is the recommended starting point for examining the business, as it is closest to the customer. To find out the true sales situation, there is no substitute for accompanying sales staff on customer visits. One can quickly find out both customer reaction and sales effectiveness.

The next area to examine should be the sale-support functions, such as the sales office, estimating department and after-sales service. Aspects to be examined should include:

▷ what credit status checks are made on prospective customers and what is the level of bad debts?

▷ how accurate are product and contract cost estimates?

▷ how competitive are prices, quantity discounts and payment terms?

▷ what are the authority and basis for quoting non-standard prices?

▷ how quickly and professionally are quotations submitted?

▷ how quick is delivery? Are sales being lost because of long delivery periods?

▷ what is the level of out-of-stock situations?

▷ what is the level of complaints and warranty claims, and how well are they handled?

▷ how quickly and effectively are telephone calls and correspondence acted upon?

Marketing

Marketing should be examined next. The knowledge gained from the sales operations should be of valuable help in assessing marketing effectiveness.

It is particularly easy for people to confuse work and results in marketing. Factual answers should be obtained to searching questions such as:

▷ how does the department measure its own effectiveness?

▷ what tangible results and contributions have been achieved?

▷ how is the effectiveness of advertising, exhibitions and other promotional activities measured?

▷ what is known in detail about the market and competition?

Manufacturing, distribution and administration should be examined next. Questions to be asked include the following:

Manufacturing

▷ how can we reduce product costs without additional capital expenditure?

▷ what is needed to reduce product costs significantly?

▷ how can reject and wastage levels be reduced?

▷ how can product quality and reliability be increased without additional cost?

▷ which production bottlenecks need to be overcome?

▷ how can delivery times be shortened with additional facilities?

▷ what small outlays of expenditure would produce substantial profit improvement speedily?

▷ how can raw-material, work-in-progress and finished-goods stocks be reduced without losing profitable sales opportunities?

▷ what surplus equipment and redundant stocks should be sold off?

Distribution

▷ how can distribution costs be reduced?

▷ how can deliveries be speeded up?

▷ what are the levels of damaged goods and items returned?

▷ how else can customer service be improved?

▷ how are peak-period requirements dealt with?

Administration

> ▷ what would happen if we stopped doing this task, or scrapped the whole department?

> ▷ why is it done daily and not weekly, or weekly instead of monthly, etc?

> ▷ could it be done less expensively in another department or location?

> ▷ what jobs are being left undone, to the detriment of the business?

Research and development

Research and development is probably, but not necessarily, the last department to be examined. Questions to be asked include:

> ▷ what proportion of the total budget is spent on:
> • fundamental research?
> • new product development?
> • improvements to existing products?

> ▷ what is the status of each current project?

> ▷ what are the market, commercial and financial arguments for continuing each project?

> ▷ what projects are planned to start in the foreseeable future?

> ▷ what tangible results have come from the department in recent years, and what failures?

At the end of this review of the company the chief executive should decide upon the level of cost reduction to be achieved in each department. A common percentage cost reduction in each department may appear to be equitable, but it is almost certainly inappropriate.

Then the head of each function should be asked to make

specific proposals for the people to be dismissed and other cost reductions to be made, for approval by the chief executive. Speed and confidentiality are important, as rumours and anxiety are inevitable.

THE SECOND MONTH

Redundancies should be announced simultaneously across the whole company, for people need to be assured and to believe that further redundancies will be unnecessary. A second round of redundancies is likely to cause lasting damage to morale.

Department managers should submit concise written profit improvement plans for immediate implementation, and give an estimate of the effect on current-year profits.

Revised budgets should be prepared quickly for the remainder of the current year. The chief executive will need to review and approve each department budget to ensure that the level of achievement proposed is sufficiently demanding.

The financial analysis which has been done will enable the monthly sales figures required to achieve a break-even position to be calculated. Every manager must be aware of the figure and a target month agreed upon as the deadline for exceeding that figure.

It must be realised, however, that eliminating losses is only the first stage of a successful turn-around. The goal must be to achieve an adequate return on the total funds invested in the business. Eliminating losses is usually the easier and quicker task. Selecting a few key tasks to be done urgently, simply and outstandingly well is often sufficient to eliminate losses. To achieve a satisfactory return on investment in a turn-around situation may require major new initiatives to be taken, particularly if there is surplus capacity in the industrial sector.

THE THIRD MONTH

By now the worst of the upheaval and disruption should be out of the way. No time must be lost in building future success. A vision statement should be written with the total commitment of the management team. Their major business development projects should be identified, and personal accountabilities assigned, as the means of translating the vision into tangible achievement.

The vision statement and business development projects need to be addressed before budget preparation for the next financial year is begun. The budget process should be particularly rigorous in order to provide a clearly thought-out operating plan for the coming financial year. The management team must realise that the agreed budget represents a collective cabinet commitment to achieve the profit and cash flow budgets.

Two of the most valuable assets for the chief executive are enthusiasm and belief. He must exude them every day, however tough the going becomes. Gradually his belief and enthusiasm will be shared by the rest of the management team.

EXECUTIVE SUMMARY

▷ Take control and make an impact on the first day

▷ Attack a cash flow crisis during the first week

▷ Assess each department and decide the initial cost reduction required during the first month

▷ Carry out any headcount reduction needed during the second month

▷ Develop a vision for future success and define major business development projects during the third month

▷ Recognise that approximate financial analysis done quickly is much more valuable than waiting for accurate figures to be produced